50 WILD PLANTS EVERYONE SHOULD KNOW

William L. Brenneman, MS MH ND

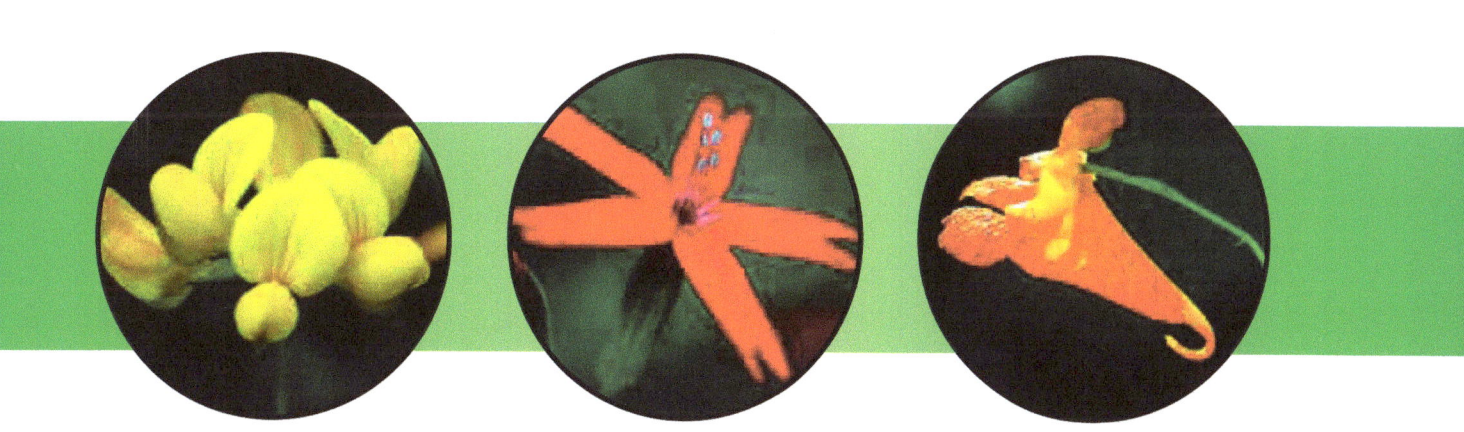

Copyright © 2022 William L. Brenneman, MS MH ND.

All rights reserved. No part of this book may be reproduced, stored, or transmitted by any means—whether auditory, graphic, mechanical, or electronic—without written permission of both publisher and author, except in the case of brief excerpts used in critical articles and reviews. Unauthorized reproduction of any part of this work is illegal and is punishable by law.

ISBN: 979-8-88640-370-1 (sc)
ISBN: 979-8-88640-371-8 (hc)
ISBN: 979-8-88640-372-5 (e)

Because of the dynamic nature of the Internet, any web addresses or links contained in this book may have changed since publication and may no longer be valid. The views expressed in this work are solely those of the author and do not necessarily reflect the views of the publisher, and the publisher hereby disclaims any responsibility for them.

One Galleria Blvd., Suite 1900, Metairie, LA 70001
1-888-421-2397

FOREWORD

Why should you know these 50 plants?

1. If you have any contact with nature, these are the plants often encountered, especially in the mid-western states.

2. These plants are part of our natural heritage – understood, utilized, and respected by pioneers and Indians.

3. Many of the plants are endangered. Many have significant health benefits. Some are a threat to the balance of nature, and need to be controlled.

4. Some have a special beauty, and have characteristics that make encounters with them a significant experience.

Certainly, many other plants could qualify to be in the "chosen 50." Perhaps feedback from readers will result in "50 More Plants Everyone Should Know." The decision was made to limit the number, and to go into more informational depth than is usually provided in a plant guide.

The plants are grouped by their most common flower color. Within each color grouping, they are arranged from earliest to latest appearing spring through fall.

To use the book for identification:
1. Find the correct flower color section
2. Check on the time of year of flowering.
3. Match the photographs carefully.

The information for each plant includes:
1. Photographs – including close-up and distant images.
2. The common name
3. The scientific name
4. Additional common names
5. The family name
6. The time of flowering by month
7. Whether the plant is <u>alien</u> (arrived in the U.S. from a foreign country) or <u>native</u> to the U.S.
8. An Introduction – highlighting unique characteristics
9. Edibility
10. Medical uses
11. Ecological relationships
12. Challenge – a hands-on activity to enhance understanding

Disclaimer: Before using any plant as food or medicine, use extreme caution and diligent research. The author and publisher assume no responsibility for adverse effects that may be encountered by using wild plants.

The information is based on over 30 years of study and experience leading hikes for all ages as a Biology instructor. This book compiles information that should be relevant to anyone interested in an introductory study of wild plants, and will be helpful in learning more about common wild plants that are most likely encountered in the woods, along roadways, in open fields or even in the back yard. The 50 plants are found throughout the mid-west and many are widespread over the entire U.S. Most of the plants chosen are herbaceous (have a soft, non-woody stem). Also included is one vine (Japanese Honeysuckle) and one shrub (Elderberry). There are no trees in the book.

An attempt has been made to limit the confusing volume of terminology included in many identification books. A glossary is provided at the back of the book.

As a Naturopath, the author has special interest in medical qualities of the plants. Many of these are the subject of ongoing scientific research. Amazing in quantity and accuracy are the uses discovered by our forefathers and Native Americans. How compelling the discussions must have been as the pioneers and Indians shared their experiences and knowledge regarding "Nature's Pharmacy." How intriguing it would be to know details of their successes and failures as they learned by trial and error. How often did errors result in harm or death? Did they really sentence prisoners to "try out" an unknown weed? We know that both groups struggled with respiratory problems: Coughs, colds, pneumonia, tuberculosis, etc. These were the leading causes of death, especially among children. Staying healthy was a constant struggle, as they existed in cold, drafty cabins or tee-pees, and worked hard year around, often in harsh weather. Finding natural cures was an on-going challenge.

Meanwhile, many of our modern pharmaceuticals have their origin in wild plants. Modern scientific techniques involve the extraction, concentration, and synthesis of the "active ingredients," found in plants. The resulting drugs are convenient, and often effective, but can have significant side effects.

Conservation considerations

"We will conserve only what we love. We will love only what we understand. We will understand only what we are taught." Baba Dioum, Senegalese environmentalist.

While many wild plants are edible and nutritious, and while many have specific health benefits, they are not being advocated here as a substantial substitute for grocery stores and pharmacies. Their use in modern society should be restrained while recognizing that the gene pool represented in nature still has the potential of providing important health benefits both now and in the future.

Perhaps for this reason alone, every community should provide a habitat conservation program to protect wildlife. While limited sampling is occasionally justified – just "picking the pretty flowers" for fun should be discouraged. Perhaps the emphasis on conserving areas like the Rain Forest needs to be balanced by concerns in our own backyards. Too many natural plants are endangered by habitat destruction.

Learning to identify wild plants, even if only 50, will make contact with nature more enjoyable, and will enhance awareness of the beauty of nature. Hopefully, we will become less likely to dismiss a wild plant as just a weed. Applying names gives a sense of being at home in the woods - of being connected with nature, and promotes feelings of belonging and reality - emotions we need in our mobile, stressful society. As we learn more about the plants, a connection develops with our planet, and those who have gone before us - our forefathers - whose very survival depended on their knowledge of nature. They felt a divine connection through these plants, and with the creator who provided them.

Often the pioneers' survival instincts superceded any conservation concerns, but perhaps they felt justified in indiscriminate use when viewing the enormity of the forest lands compared to the relative sparse size of the human population at that time in our history.

Only the most thoughtful and insightful of our ancestors could have predicted the long-range impact of over-use, and their practice of importing plants from one country to another. Many of the plants (16 of the 50) that are so abundant in our environment were not here a century ago, and their impact continues to be an ecological challenge. We can only attempt to understand why our forefathers

chose not to leave their homelands without bringing along samples of their favorite herbs. Meanwhile, visiting foreign Botanists have been amazed at the variety of wild plants in this country, and the overall disregard for habitat preservation.

Challenge

Make a goal to learn to identify all 50 of the plants. Many can be found along roadsides, in open fields, and in any forest. Learning their names, and knowing something about these common plants takes practice and effort, but provides a sense of satisfaction and connection with the plants.

Once all 50 are mastered, you may be motivated to consult the more comprehensive and technical books that are in any bookstore. References are listed in the bibliography.

Remember to limit picking, and admire without disturbing. Consider investing in a close-up lens, and collect with a camera (take pictures, not plants)

Encourage your local school to set-up a nature study area. Outdoor labs should be an integral part of any school system.

Perhaps Edward W. Bok's grandmother has given each of us the ultimate challenge. In her words: "Make you the world a bit better or more beautiful because you have lived in it."

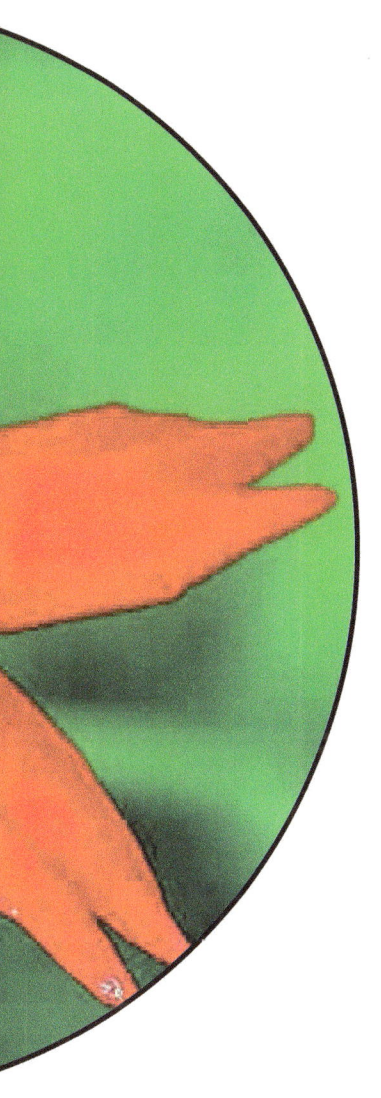

CONTENTS

Foreword / iii

Alphabetical Listing of Plants / ix

White Flowers / 1

Yellow Flowers / 29

Maroon, Red, Pink Flowers / 45

Purple, Violet Flowers / 59

Blue Flowers / 65

Green Flowers / 73

Orange Flowers / 89

Glossary / 93

References / 95

Reviews / 97

ALPHABETICAL LISTING OF PLANTS

Aster
Birdsfoot Trefoil
Bloodroot
Butterfly weed
Cattail
Chicory
*Clover, Red
Daisy Fleabane
*Dandelion
Dutchman's Breeches
Elderberry
Evening Primrose
Fire Pink
*Garlic Mustard
Garlic, *Field and Wild
Ginger
Goldenrod
Hepatica
Horsetail
Ironweed
Jack-in-the-Pulpit
Japanese Honeysuckle
Jewelweed
Joe-pye weed
Lobelia
Mayapple
Milkweed – Common and Swamp

*Mullein
*Oxeye Daisy
Phlox, Blue
Poison Hemlock
*Poison Ivy
Pokeweed
Ragweed - Common and Giant
Ragwort
Rue Anemone
Snakeroot
Solomon's Seal
Spring Beauty
Squirrel Corn
*Stinging Nettle
Thistle – Field, *Bull, *Canada
Toothwort
Trillium, Large Flowered
Trillium, Prairie
Trout Lily
Violet
*Wild Carrot
Wild Geranium
Wild Onion
*Wild Parsnip
*Wood Sorrel
*Yarrow

*alien

WHITE FLOWERS

Spring Beauty

Hepatica

Bloodroot

Rue Anemone

Dutchman's Breeches

*Japanese Honeysuckle

*Garlic Mustard

Squirrel Corn

Large Flowered Trillium

Toothwort

May Apple

*Wild Carrot

Daisy Fleabane

*Poison Hemlock

Elderberry

*Yarrow

*Ox-eye Daisy

Pokeweed

Snakeroot

Aster

*Alien

50 Wild Plants Everyone Should Know

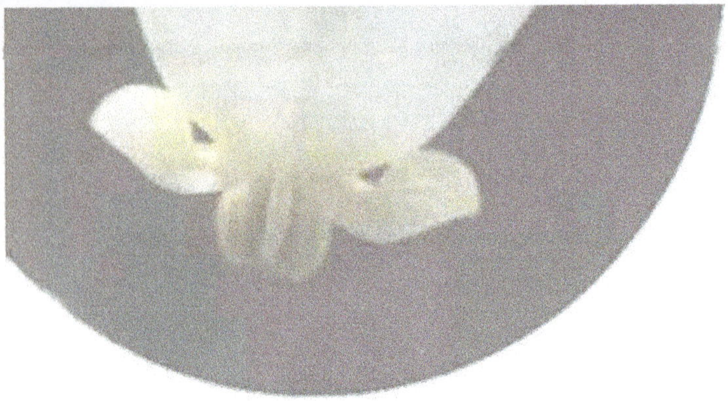

SPRING BEAUTY

Claytonia Virginica
Family: Purslane
March - May

Native

Other Names
Fairy Spuds
Wild Potato

Description
The beautiful display of Spring Beauty flowers carpeting the forest floor announces the arrival of spring. Delicate clusters of pink- veined, starry blossoms are supported by wiry stems, and are nestled in fleshy, grass-like foliage. Spreading like a pink mist over the landscape, they resemble a spring snowfall. Pioneer children struggled to dig up the roots - their underground snack. The little "potatoes" with protruding eyes are up to 1" in diameter. They were eaten raw (radish flavor) boiled (potato flavor) or roasted (chestnut flavor). They should be gathered sparingly, because digging up the roots destroys a beautiful, scented flower cluster, which can produce up to fifteen blossoms.

Edibility
The roots taste best if boiled in salty water 10 – 15 minutes. They are up to 3" deep, and should be dug out of the ground- not pulled. To find the largest roots, look for clumps of many stems growing together. Removing the brown skin will improve the taste. Foliage is grazed by deer.

Medicinal / Nutritional
Bulbs are high in vitamins A and C. Cherokees consumed the entire plant and considered it a form of birth control.

Ecology
The white to pink flowers have two sepals and five petals. They attract over 70 kinds of insects. Petals tend to close under heavy shade and clouds. They are pollinated by small bees.

Challenge
Dig (don't pull) a tuber from under a flower cluster for a taste test. Is it more like a radish or potato?

50 Wild Plants Everyone Should Know

HEPATICA

Hepatica Americana
Family: Poppy
March – May

Native

Other Names
Liver Leaf

Challenge
Determine which of two species are encountered: round lobed or sharp lobed. Round lobed are found more to the north and prefer acid soil. Sharp lobed are more in the south and prefer basic soil. The two species may be found in the same area, and they will hybridize.

Description
Stimulated by just a few warm days, hepatica bursts from last year's ever-green leaves early in the spring into beautiful clusters of fragrant, bluish, or white blossoms with striking yellow and white centers, and supported by shiny, silky stems. The dark, leathery three lobed leaves are liver-shaped. They will be replaced, after flowering, with new spotted, light green leaves that will last through the next winter. Some say they are the most beautiful early spring wild flower, and they are popular in rock gardens.

Edibility
A tea can be made from the new leaves: one ounce of dried leaves to one pint of boiling water.

Medicinal / Nutritional
Best known as a liver tonic – the lobed leaves have the shape of the human liver, and this was considered a clue to its use.(The belief that, if a plant structure resembled the shape of a specific human organ, it would be therapeutic to that organ, was known as the "Doctrine of Signatures.") In the late 1800's, the tea became very popular for liver ailments, but its effectiveness is now controversial. The tea was also used for treating freckles and sunburn.

Meskwaki medicine man quote: "When the mouth gets twisted, and the eyes get crossed, brew the root into a tea and wash the face."

Ecology
It will grow in deep shade or full sun, and in a wide variety of soils. Ants assist in seed dispersal.

BLOODROOT

Sanguinaria Canadensis
Family: Poppy
March – May

Native

Other Names
Indian Paint
Puccoon

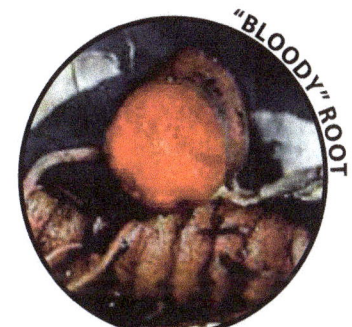
"BLOODY" ROOT

BLOODROOT SEEDS

Description
One of the first spring wild flowers to bloom- the plant emerges as a single leaf which curls around the bud. Then a white flower blooms with intricately designed petals and a vivid golden-orange center. The flower closes at night, and drops its petals after a week. The attractive, bluish green, deeply cut leaf, unfurls and lasts into the summer. Bloodroot is best known for its thick root, found 1-2" below ground, which if cut, "bleeds" blood red and will stain anything, including skin. The Ponca Indian braves rubbed the root juice on their palm as a love charm. Then they tried to shake hands with their desired squaw who would "usually" agree to marriage within a week.

Edibility
The root is considered poisonous, and contains an alkaloid related to morphine. Consumption may cause tunnel vision.

Medicinal / Nutritional
Indian usage: wart removal, decorative skin and cloth dye, war paint, insect repellant and permanent wood stain.

Modern usage: Has been grown commercially as an FDA approved ingredient in mouth wash and toothpaste (including Viadent) to inhibit tooth plaque. It is effective, but may cause mouth lesions. The root contains both sanguinarine (anti-inflammatory) and berberine (anti-bacterial), and research continues for promising usage to control: cancer, (including brain tumors) bronchial and throat infections, heart problems, and skin diseases. It is being used as an alternative to surgery for the removal of skin growths such as moles and warts. The affect is rapid, and normal skin tissue is not harmed. Bloodroot paste preparations are available at natural health companies.

Ecology
Ants gather the seeds, consume the seed cover, and widely distribute the unharmed seeds. Bloodroot is considered endangered, but responds well to transplantation and cultivation.

Challenge:
How many petals does Bloodroot have? (usually 8 – up to 16). If a cluster of plants is found, choose one, carefully dig up the root and observe the "blood".

RUE ANEMONE

Anemonella thalictroides
Family: Buttercup
March – May

Native

Other Names
Wind flower

Challenge
Count the petal-like sepals. If there are six to ten, you have found Rue Anemone. If there are only five, it is called False Rue Anemone.

Description
Early in spring, beds of bright green, ankle high, mitten shaped leaves produce beautiful pearl shaped buds and bright white blossoms on wiry flexible stems that tremble at the slightest breeze (wind flower) announcing that "spring is here." Whorls of three lobed leaves support the delicate umbrella-like, white to pinkish petals surrounding the pistils and the tiny, bright, yellow anthers.

Edibility
Some plants have clusters of tuberous roots which were used for food by Indians and pioneers. Known as wild potatoes, they are now considered slightly poisonous.

Medicinal / Nutritional
Indians considered the root tea a cure-all: used for diarrhea, vomiting, headaches, gout, leprosy, and to soothe the throat for singing.

Ecology
Flowers are wind pollinated. Ants eat seed casings and spread the seeds. In some areas it is becoming endangered.

DUTCHMAN'S-BREECHES

Dicentra cucullaria
Family: Poppy
March – May

Native

Other Names
Staggerweed
Ear Drops

POISONOUS TUBERS

Description
This plant is often confused with Squirrel Corn – the leaves and flowers are similar. However, Squirrel Corn flowers are described as heart-shaped, where-as Dutchman flowers resemble up-side-down bloomer pants – worn by Dutchmen, complete with yellow tips representing the belt. There are up to ten creamy, white inflated flowers dangling on slender stalks above the leaf canopy resembling white-lanterned towers. They sometimes appear as a row of molar teeth

Edibility
Roots, stems and leaves are poisonous. Cattle and horses will graze on leaves and sometimes pull up and eat the pinkish tubers causing them to tremble, stagger and gasp for breath – a condition known as blue staggers.

Medicinal / Nutritional
Native Americans found a way to use the plant to treat syphilis. Iroquois made a liniment of boiled roots that they used to limber their legs for running.

Ecology
Like squirrel corn, pollination is by bumblebees. Smaller bees chew holes in the flower to rob the nectar. Seeds are spread by ants.

Challenge
Look for insect holes in flowers. Look closely at the flower shape. Are they more like pants, lanterns or teeth?

JAPANESE HONEYSUCKLE

Lonicera japonica
Family: Honeysuckle
April - July

Alien (Asia)

Other Names
Gold and Silver Flower
Woodbine
Chin Yin Hua

Challenge
Pull apart some flowers, find and taste a drop of the honey-flavored nectar at the base of the petals.
What would you say to someone who says: "I like this plant, and I am going to grow it on an arbor, but I won't let it spread."
Do your part to control it. Pull out a vine by the root. Try weaving the vine into a small wreath or basket.

6 JAPANESE HONEYSUCKLE

Description
Our relationship to this alien vine is one of contrasts: Its medical qualities can save human lives, but aggressive growth can destroy entire natural habitats, including native trees and shrubs. Introduced from Japan in 1806 in New York, it was valued as an ornamental, for erosion control and ground cover, and for its medicinal qualities. While slow to become aggressive, by the early 1900's it had spread into most states, and is now considered a harmful invasive. However, the original uses remain, and it is still sold in nurseries.

The white flowers quickly fade to yellow. They are full of nectar, and have an "unbelievable fragrance." The flowers produce green, then black berries, which are consumed by birds resulting in wide seed distribution. The root creeps quickly underground and sends up stems that can climb brick walls and trees – up to 80 feet – shading, choking, bending, and breaking with sheer weight, anything in its path. Once established, control is very difficult – even using a specifically designed removal tool – the honeysuckle popper, which pulls out the roots. The vine emerges from under trash and even brick piles. It seems to need no care and has few natural enemies - although deer will eat it. Even its national counterpart – the Japanese Beetle, ignores it. The hairy vine stem turns woody but remains flexible with age, and is used to make durable baskets and decorative wreaths. The flower fragrance is so special that the plants are used as a potpourri.

Edibility
The buds and flowers are edible, and have been used to make syrup and pudding. Leaves are boiled and used as a vegetable. Leaves and flowers are used for a healthful beverage tea.

OVER-GROWING A SMALL TREE

Medicinal / Nutritional

The flower tea has a long history of use in Asia to treat sore throat, fever, flu and hepatitis. It is anti-viral, anti-bacterial, and lowers cholesterol and blood pressure.

Externally it is used as a wash to relieve arthritis and breast cancer. There is a high content of magnesium, calcium and potassium.

Ecology

It prefers the southern states, and severe cold weather will restrict growth. The leaves tend to be evergreen. Pollination is by the sphinx moth. It is spread by birds attracted to the glossy, black berries. They deposit seeds over a wide area. It has become a serious threat to native plants by spreading into woodlands, as the vine can wrap around and strangle anything in its path. It can tolerate some shade and usually penetrates a forest after becoming established along the edge of the tree line.

It provides food and cover for many species of wildlife.

GARLIC MUSTARD

GARLIC MUSTARD

Alliaria petiolata
Family: Mustard
April – June

Alien – Europe

Other Names
Poor Man's Mustard
Jack-in-the-Bush

Challenge
Discover the garlic smell by crushing or nibbling on the leaves. Do the forest a favor: carefully pull up the plants – including roots, and remove from the area in plastic bags.

Description
Well-meaning European settlers could not have known the ecological havoc this plant would cause after escaping their gardens. Since first appearing in 1868 in Long Island, New York, it has spread into the woodlands of at least 38 states and Canada. The pioneers valued it as a tasty, healthful pot-herb. In Europe, growth is controlled by many natural enemies – over 60 insects consume it. In the U.S. it seems to be enemy free – even deer will not eat it. Because of the ability to spread so rapidly, it is becoming a major threat to our native plants – including trees.

Effective control is very difficult. All over the country, environmental groups organize "hunt and pull" programs, and carry it out in bags from infested woodlands. Efforts are even made to control it by reviving interest in its original use – food and health benefits. In Maryland there are contests for ways to make it edible. Recipes have been submitted for use in ravioli, pesto, corn bead, and pasta. It is biennial. The shiny black seeds sprout into a ground-hugging rosette, which remains green all winter. It grows quickly, up to three feet tall, and has triangular or heart-shaped leaves, and clusters of white flowers with four cross-shaped petals. By May, up to 8,000 seeds are released from slender brown pods. Plants have been found to advance across a woodlot over 100 feet per year.

OVER-TAKING A WOODLOT

Edibility
Young leaves can be used in any recipe calling for mustard greens. They can be used in salad or boiled and served like spinach. Seeds are a pepper substitute. The long roots from large plants can be sliced and used like horse radish.

Medicinal / Nutritional
It is high in vitamins A and C and aids digestion. Preparations have been used to treat gangrene and ulcers.

Ecology
Because of the size and rapid growth, it can out compete and replace any of our native plants. This deprives wildlife of food: nectar, fruit, seeds and roots. Seeds live for five years, and it can sprout from fragments of roots. It thrives on basic soil and does not grow well in acidic soils or full sun. It has been found to disrupt the relationship between native hard-wood tree seedlings and soil fungi, thus inhibiting the growth of the young trees. Research continues on finding a "safe" foreign insect to introduce as a natural control.

SQUIRREL CORN

Dicentra Canadensis
Family: Poppy
April – May

Native

Other Names
Colic Weed
Turkey Pea
Bleeding Heart

Description
The name comes from the perennial root system which consists of orange-yellow pea sized tubers that resemble corn kernels. They are mildly poisonous, but a favorite food of mice and squirrels. The fern-like leaves are somewhat poisonous to grazing cattle. The heart shaped flowers (with "feet and a tail") resemble their "bleeding heart" relatives. The flower stalk rises and arches gracefully above the leaves and supports the white flower pendants – sometimes tinged with pink.

Medicinal / Nutritional
There are no known uses in the U.S. In Europe it was used to treat skin problems, syphilis, and menstrual problems.

Ecology
Flowers are pollinated only by bumblebees which have mouth parts long enough to reach the nectar. Smaller bees snip a hole through the flower to rob the nectar, but do nothing for pollination.

Challenge
Smell the flowers. They are very fragrant. Find a flower that has been robbed of its nectar (holes in petals). Compare the leaves of Squirrel Corn and Dutchman's Breeches. Some say that they are indistinguishable.

9 TRILLIUM

LARGE-FLOWERED TRILLIUM

TRILLIUM

Trillium sp.
Family: Lily
April – June

Native

Other Names
Birthroot

DROOPING TRILLIUM

YELLOW TRILLIUM

Description
Large-Flowered Trillium is perhaps our largest, most striking wild flower. All of the plant parts are in three's. The large waxy-white, wavy edged blossom tends to turn pink with age. It takes up to six years for the bloom to appear. While tempting to pick, restraint is in order, as it definitely deserves protection. Other species have yellow or maroon petals- see Prairie Trillium.

Other white trilliums, with smaller flowers that bend towards the ground are called Nodding or Drooping Trillium.

Edibility
Young leaves are good in salads; however, removing them will kill the plant. Native Americans believed that they made a powerful love potion if eaten.

Medicinal / Nutritional
Native Americans made a tea from the large root (rhizome) to induce childbirth and to relieve menstrual pain.

They also applied crushed leaves and blossoms to skin sores and insect bites, and ground the roots to rub on aching, rheumatic joints.

Ecology
Floral scent ranges from very pleasant to the smell of something dead. Bees pollinate the pleasant smelling blossoms, while beetles and flies prefer the foul smelling flowers.

Challenge
Smell a blossom. Would it attract bees or beetles? How many sets of three's can you find on the plant? You should find at least four sets: sepals, petals, leaves, and the top of the pistils. (stigmas)

50 Wild Plants Everyone Should Know

TOOTHWORT – CUT-LEAVED

Dentaria laciniata
Family: Mustard
April – May

Native

Other Names
Pepper-root

Challenge
Cautiously bite on a leaf. Be careful, it can be quite peppery. Try to find the string of tooth-shaped roots by carefully digging under the plant.

Description
The name comes from the slightly closed flowers that resemble teeth, and the ivory roots look like a row of tooth-shaped pop beads. They were a food source for the extinct Passenger Pigeon. The roots are shallow and parallel to the ground surface. When fully open, the petals resemble a cross, and they bloom around Easter.

The fragrant petals turn pink with age and produce long, thin seedpods. The beautiful clusters of blooms seem to herald the end of winter, and the beginning of spring. When their season is over, the finger-shaped leaves turn yellow, and the plant quickly disappears.

Edibility
The small root tubers are edible raw or cooked, and were used as a seasoning in soup. If chewed, they have a peppery, radish flavor.

Medicinal / Nutritional
Indians chewed on the roots to treat toothache and as a cold medicine. Iroquois used it as a hunting medicine by rubbing the roots on traps. They also carried roots in their pockets as a "love medicine." They rubbed crushed roots on their head to treat headaches.

Ecology
The plant is a host to the orange-tip butterfly. The flower nectar attracts many kinds of bees.

MAY-APPLE

Podophyllum peltatum
Family: Barberry
April – June

Native

Other Names
Racoon Berry
Wild Lemon
Indian Apple
American Mandrake

"MANDRAKE" ROOT

Description
Usually found in large dense patches of umbrella-like leaves (sometimes concealing the elusive morel mushroom). The first year plant has one leaf and no flower or fruit. The second year, there are two leaves and a large sweet-smelling flower grows between the leaves. The fruit turns from green to lemon yellow by fall. Some people develop a skin rash from handling the foliage and green fruits.

Edibility
The ripened fruits are popular with turtles and raccoons, and are hard to find. Pioneers enjoyed the strawberry-mango flavor. However, eating too many has a laxative effect –especially if not ripe. Fruits have been used for sauce, marmalade and cake. Dried fruits have a "delicious" aroma, and are used as a sachet. The poisonous, bitter leaves are seldom eaten by animals.

Medicinal / Nutritional
Indians ground the dried rhizomes into powder, and mixed it in water for a laxative to remove parasites. However, the powder is poisonous and too strong to self-medicate. The rhizome contains podophylin, which has anti-tumor properties. May-apple is being evaluated for growing commercially for its use as an insecticide, and treatment for venereal warts, testicular cancer, and leukemia.

Ecology
The flowers are pollinated by bumblebees. The root sometimes has a leg-like fork with a genital-like protuberance – hence the name "Mandrake."

Challenge
Locate and smell the flower found under the leaves. Do you see more single leaf, one-year plants, or double leaf, two-year plants?

WILD CARROT

Daucus carota
Family: Parsley
May - October

Alien - Native of the Mediterranean area. It was brought here by the settlers.

Other Names
Queen Anne's Lace
Birds Nest

Challenge
Smell and describe the odor of the flower. Perhaps a mixture of perfume and rubber tires?
Try to find the tiny purple floret in the middle of the flower cluster. Crush and smell a leaf, and detect the carrot odor.

WILD CARROT — 12

Description
Queen Anne of England (1700's) was so fond of this flower that it became known as Queen Ann's Lace. She used it in bouquets and as a headdress. Perhaps she was aware that if the cut stems are placed in colored water, the flower will turn that color.

As a biennial, the seed produces only ground level, fern-like foliage and a tap root the first year. The second year the stem grows up to seven feet tall and produces flat, lacy flowers. After pollination, the flower curls inward forming a hollow cup. Then It turns brown and looks like a bird's nest. Many spiny seeds form inside the nest.

Our cultivated garden carrot was produced from wild carrot by selective breeding, seed selection, and cultivation. The young first year root is edible, but is small, white, and woody.

Edibility
Coffee substitute can be made from the chopped, dried roots.

If cows eat the foliage, their milk has an unpleasant taste.

The flowers can be french-fried, and they make an attractive carrot flavored dish.

GARDEN CARROT ANCESTOR

SEED POD

PURPLE FLORET

Medicinal / Nutritional

Carrot seed tea is made by pouring a pint of boiling water over two tablespoons of crushed seeds. The tea has many health benefits including sugar digestion, and reduction of body gas.

Leaf tea strengthens the bladder and kidneys. Dried seeds have long been used as a contraceptive. Chewing on them several days after coitus releases a substance that prevents a fertilized egg from embedding.

In the middle of the white, lacy flower, a single purple floret can be found which may attract insects. A legend in England claims that consuming it will control epilepsy.

Judging by the abundance of phyto-nutrients found in this plant, there may be significant health promoting potential yet to be discovered

Ecology

Over 60 kinds of insects are attracted to the flower. Leaves are savored by Black Swallowtail caterpillars,

DAISY FLEABANE

Erigeron annuus
Family: Composite
May – October

Native – has spread to Europe

Other Names
Lace Buttons

Challenge
Try to find two of its favorite inhabitants: inchworms, and the tiny crab spider, which hides behind the flower and captures insect visitors.

Description
This is the original, natural daisy from which the larger common daisies were developed. While often dismissed as a weed, the cheerful flower is an important link in insect ecology. It grows up to five feet with one-half inch wide flowers. The numerous "petals" are actually ray flowers – each an individual flower.

Edibility
The plant is a favorite of sheep and deer. Nectar and pollen attract many insects.

Medicinal / Nutritional
The name is from its past use as a flea repellent. Dried plants were hung from a bed post or even stuffed into mattresses. There is no scientific support of its effectiveness.

Daisy tea is a folk remedy for diarrhea, fever and bronchitis.

Ecology
As a winter annual, seeds sprout in late summer and it over-winters as a rosette of green leaves. It is very drought resistant, and can become invasive on farm land.

POISON HEMLOCK

POISON HEMLOCK

Conium maculatum
Family: Parsley
June – August

Alien – Europe

Other Names
Poison Parsley

Description
One of the world's most poisonous plants, Hemlock was used in ancient Greece to kill convicted prisoners, including the famous philosopher, Socrates. He was charged with disrespecting the religious traditions in Athens, and was made to drink a fatal cup of hemlock tea. Hemlock was brought to this country as an ornamental, with its attractive, large, lacy leaves, and delicate white flower clusters. Here it has found a home along roadsides, edges of fields and railroads. The flower is sometimes mistaken for wild carrot, but it has smooth, purple-spotted stems, whereas wild carrot has "hairy" stems and leaves. It is a biennial, and grows up to ten feet tall the second year.

Indians dipped arrow tips into the poisonous stem juice. The juice is believed to be in the cup given to Christ on the cross.

Edibility
All parts are poisonous, especially young leaves and seeds. All grazing animals are affected, especially sheep, causing trembling, bloating and suffocation. The quality and taste of dairy cattle milk can be altered. Butterflies are attracted to the flower nectar.

Medicinal / Nutritional
It has been used by Herbalists as an antispasmodic (muscle spasms) to treat arthritis. However, there is a delicate balance between a therapeutic amount and a poisonous affect.

Ecology
Seeds are spread by birds in the winter. The only natural control appears to be the larvae of a light green moth from Europe, which feeds on the leaves. It sometimes invades alfalfa and grain fields

Challenge
Use extreme caution when near the plant – not advisable to make flower bouquets! The leaves have a musty, mouse-like odor. Look for the red or purple stem spots - said to represent the blood of Socrates.

ELDERBERRY

Sambucus Canadensis
Family: Honeysuckle
June – August

Native

Other Names
Pipe Tree

Challenge
Smell the flowers – some say they have a "strange" odor. Taste (don't swallow) a ripe berry from different shrubs. There can be a big difference in sweetness. Cut off a six inch section of the stem - observe the soft inner pith. Punch it out and after thoroughly washing and drying – construct a flute or whistle.

Description
The small, seedy, juicy, blue-black berries are a nutrition powerhouse, sometimes called "the medicine chest of the common people." The name may refer to its use by "elders" to maintain their youth. It grows as a shrub, up to twelve feet tall, and has large compound leaves with starry, white, lacy flower clusters up to six inches across. It prefers rich, wet soil and is found in marshes, riverbanks, and roadsides. Crumpled leaves can be spread in a garden as a natural insecticide. The stems contain unusual soft, white pith which can be pushed out with a sharp stick. Sections of these hollowed stems have been used to make: whistles, straws, "pea" shooters, maple syrup spikes (elder quill), flutes, pipes, and to blow air while starting a fire. Caution must be used with mouth contact, as the stem is considered poisonous. Kids have been poisoned by blowing on hand-made flutes and "pop-guns."

Edibility
Flowers make delicious fritters. Dip flower clusters into a light batter and fry. Combine with mint to make a healthy tea.

Berries are best not used raw, as they are sweet, but bland and slightly toxic. Strip ripe purple berries from the stem with a fork or coarse comb, or freeze for easy removal from stems. Use in muffins, bread, cake, jam, homemade wine, ice cream, and apple pie (60% apples, 40% berries)

The berries are a valuable wild-life food. Over forty kinds of birds consume the seeds.

STEM WITH PITH REMOVED

Medicinal / Nutritional
Berries are very high in Vitamin C and contain A and B vitamins, amino acids, potassium, and calcium. A berry extract called Sambucol (health stores) is very effective in treating colds and flu. Our forefathers found medical uses for all parts of the plant, and treated virtually every body ailment (up to 70 diseases) including asthma, back pain, constipation and arthritis. The leaves and flowers were made into ointments for burns, cuts, and swellings. Crushed leaves can be rubbed on the skin to repel insects.

Ecology
The shrub lives up to five years. New sprouts will grow from the roots. Seeds are distributed by birds. It is a host of the Cecropia, our largest moth. While preferring rich, damp soil, it will adapt to poor, dry soil and is often seen in roadside ditches.

YARROW

Achillea millefolium
Family: Composite
June – October

Alien – brought by pioneers from Europe

Other Names
Little Feather
Squirrel Tail
Old Man's Pepper

"FEATHER LEAF"

Challenge
Crush and smell the unique odor of the leaf or flower. You may notice a resemblance to Listerine. It quickly relieves a stuffy nose. Legend: Wrap the plant in cloth and place under your pillow to induce "prophetic love dreams."

Description
Yarrow should be regarded with special respect, even reverence, with consideration to the thousands of lives it has saved and healed over its long history of use. Crushing and inhaling a feathery, fern-like leaf perhaps reveals a clue to its uniqueness - a curious odor from a synergistic blend of hundreds of phyto-chemicals. The application of these therapeutic chemicals, whether discovered through trial and error or research, runs the gamut of human maladies. Many herbalists would choose yarrow, if they were limited to the use of only one herb. Yet from a modern perspective, it is largely ignored and dismissed as a common weed. It is frequently found in sunny fields with its densely packed, flat, white flower clusters and leaves that appear as feathers.

The scientific name is from Achilles, the Greek war hero, who learned that the bleeding of wounded soldiers could be quickly stopped when crushed leaves were applied to an injury.

From seed, a ground-level rosette of feather-like leaves is formed (similar to wild carrot). The second year it produces a flower stalk (up to three feet tall). In the fall, the flower stem dries, but the underground stem (rhizome) survives the winter – so it is considered a perennial. In the spring, new stems arise from the rhizomes and form dense colonies. The flower stalks are popular in dried plant arrangements. Colorful horticultural variants are popular in flower gardens.

Edibility
Tea is made by infusing two teaspoons of finely chopped leaves and/or flowers in a cup of boiling water for fifteen minutes. Cooked young leaves have a spinach-like sweet, slightly bitter taste.

If cows graze on it, their milk tends to become bitter.

Medicinal / Nutritional

Medicinal benefits are derived from consuming or applying the tea infusion. The flowers are the most medicinally active, and they are high in vitamins and minerals, including magnesium, calcium, phosphorus and vitamin C.

In general, it is very beneficial for the body systems of circulation, digestion and excretion.

Preparations can be used to relieve excess mucous involving allergies, asthma, hay fever, colds and flu. It may promote perspiration thus relieving fever. (Gargle for sore throat.)

It is a blood stimulator – improving circulation and high blood pressure. Soak a pad in a solution and apply to varicose veins and eczema – a very smoothing skin wash.

It regulates menstruation, contains salicylic acid (aspirin), reduces fever and pain, and is used to relieve arthritis, rheumatism, diarrhea, and gout.

It is anti-tumor, and is active against leukemia cells. It has been used as a shampoo for dandruff and to prevent baldness. Chewing on leaves will relieve toothache. Inhaling crushed leaves relieves sinus congestion. Rubbing crushed leaves over the skin will repel mosquitoes.

It is a good companion plant in gardens as it tends to attract lady bugs and stinging insects, but repels most others, including Japanese Beetles. Root secretions make plants disease resistant. When grown with wheat, the quality and quantity of the yield is increased.

The leaf structure functions as a high frequency, short wave antennae, which may protect against some forms of radiation.

OX-EYE DAISY

Chrysanthemum leucanthemum
Family: Composite
June – August

Alien-from Europe

Other Names
Moon Penny
Dog Daisy
Gools

Challenge
Cautiously smell the flower, or crushed leaf. Some say the aroma is pleasant - some say nasty. Look for a tiny black centipede that lives only in Ox-eye flowers.

Description
A plant both loved and hated. It has an attractive flower with large white flower petals, and looks nice in cut flower arrangements. You can even eat the flowers, or prepare a leaf tea that will relieve a cough. For these reasons, the settlers chose to bring them here from Europe. However, the large yellow and white flower head can produce up to 26,000 seeds, and the underground stem can spread rapidly so that dense stands will quickly take over a sunny field, such as a cow pasture, and endanger native plants. Even animals disagree. The flowers are relished by sheep, goats and horses, but avoided by cows, pigs and deer. If cows do eat them, their milk has a bad taste. Ox - eye daisy is a persistent perennial, and is resistant to most herbicides. Forty three states list it as a noxious weed.

Edibility
Flowers and young leaves are edible – usually used in salads. Flower buds can be marinated or pickled.

Medicinal / Nutritional
Ox-eye leaf tea relaxes the bronchioles, and is a home remedy for coughs, asthma, and stomach ulcers. It will bring healing to wounds, if crushed flowers and leaves are applied as a poultice.

Ecology
The flower of some species contains pyrethrum, a chemical which repels insects and is used in organic insecticides.

In poor soil, the stem is short and sturdy. In rich soil, it grows up to three feet tall, and has a weak stem that tends to fall over. It is most prolific after a cold winter.

18 POKEWEED

POKEWEED

Phytolacca Americana
Family: Pokeweed
July – September

Native

Other Names
Pigeon Berry
Cancer-root

Description
Truly a unique perennial; growth is up to ten feet tall with tropical-like large, heart shaped leaves, and hollow, purplish-red stems. Large drooping white flower clusters produce green, then, dimpled purple berries, (as if they have been "poked").

There are many claims to fame:
Used by Indians to "cast out evil spirits. Consuming berries sometimes causes diarrhea and vomiting which the Indians felt cleansed the body. They used the juice as a dye to decorate horses, and to stain garments and feathers.

Helped elect a president: James K. Polk. Sometimes Poke was spelled Polk, and supporters wore pieces of the purple stem.

Henry Thoreau was fond of using the stiff, purple stem as a walking stick.

Pioneers wrote many letters and documents with pokeberry ink.. Civil war letters are still legible.

Juice was added to pale wines to give them color.

Inspired the writing of "Poke Salad Annie" sung by Elvis Presley, about a poor Southern girl who picked pokeweed for a vegetable

Harlan, Kentucky has a Poke Sallet Festival, and there is a Polk Salad Association in Tennessee.

Challenge
Dip a pointed stick into the berry juice and try writing with it. Be careful to keep juice off skin. It can be irritating, and is a permanent stain.

Edibility
Young stem shoots and leaves are delicious and nutritious (boiled twice) and are sold in markets – called Poke sallet. Cooking breaks down and leaches the toxins.

Children are attracted to the purple berries. The fruit is not poisonous, but the seeds are very poisonous. One man consumed twenty-five berries safely, but was careful to spit out the seeds.

Grazing animals will not eat it. Birds eagerly consume the sometimes fermented berries, and become intoxicated or drugged and then fly out of control. They were a favorite of the extinct Passenger Pigeon. Juice causes bird's body waste to have a distinct purple color, which is freely and widely distributed along with the seeds.

Medicinal / Nutritional
It is an effective, but powerful natural remedy - best left to professionals. Research is on- going, with significant potential regarding: breast cancer, leukemia, Herpes, HIV, arthritis, swollen glands, bronchitis, acne, etc.

Ecology
The seeds are scattered by birds. Therefore it is often found along fence rows. It attracts butterflies, and can be pollinated by ants.

The stem dies in the fall then re-grows from the perennial root in the spring.

19 SNAKEROOT, WHITE

SNAKEROOT, WHITE

Eupatorium rugosum
Ageratina altissima
Family: Composite
July – October

Native

Other Names
Rich Weed
White Sanick

Challenge
Admire with respect from afar, and avoid contact.

Description
Snakeroot blooms in late summer and into the fall. The attractive flower clusters are snowy white, fuzzy, and fragrant. Growth is up to three feet tall with oval, toothed, heart-shaped leaves. There are three main veins on the underside of the leaf.

Snakeroot is responsible for the death of Abraham Lincoln's mother - Nancy Hanks Lincoln. She died in 1818 from drinking infected milk not long after the family had moved to Southern Indiana. She was not alone. In the early 1800's, thousands died of the mysterious milk sickness. The disease remained a frontier mystery for over one hundred years. Then in 1928, a USDA researcher isolated trematol (an alcohol) from snakeroot, and discovered that it was in the milk of cows grazing on snakeroot. It causes cows to have muscle trembling, a stiff gait, and heart failure. Today, most dairymen are aware, and protect cattle from contact.

The leaves are bitter, and avoided by most herbivores, but it can affect all grazing animals and their nursing young.

Edibility
WARNING: Toxic - contains poisonous chemicals – potentially fatal if consumed.

Medicinal
The name comes from the use of the thick root as a poultice to treat snake bite, although its effectiveness has not been confirmed. Animals bitten by a poisonous snake have been known to chew on the root.

Ecology
Snakeroot is a perennial and spreads under-ground, preferring forest edges and disturbed areas. The nectar and pollen attract many insects. Its presence is a good reason for keeping livestock from grazing in a wooded area.

ASTER

Aster species
Family: Composite
August – October

Native

Other Names
Frost Flower
Starwort

Challenge
Observe the center of the flower. If it has not been pollinated, the floral structures will be yellow. After pollination, the color changes to rose, purple or brown.

Description
There are hundreds of species, and they all look like little daisies. Perhaps the most attractive is the purple New England Aster. The white-flowered species look like stars sprinkled along the landscape. They are perennials, but live with annuals and bloom and brighten the autumn landscape when annuals are dying. They can withstand frost, and provide the last chance for bees to obtain nectar and pollen. They are attractive in dried plant arrangements. In the past, they were thought to have special powers, and were placed around church alters to control evil spirits. The flower head is one half to one inch wide.

Edibility
Indians cooked and ate young leaves.

Medicinal
Indians used leaf tea for headaches. They used New England Aster root tea to treat diarrhea and fever.

Ecology
Asters reproduce and spread rapidly by seeds and underground stems. They grow into colonies and cover large disturbed areas.

Many butterfly and moth larvae depend on aster for food – some exclusively.

YELLOW FLOWERS

Trout Lily, Dogtooth Violet

*Dandelion

Ragwort

*Yellow Wood Sorrel

*Birds-foot Trefoil

*Wild Parsnip

*Mullein

Evening Primrose

Golden Rod

*Alien

21 TROUT LILY

Description
From deep in the soil, tooth-shaped roots produce pointed purple leaves that emerge eagerly through the ground surface or even melting snow - forming a ground cover as if a trunk-less tree, repeating an annual ritual that may pre-date the surrounding trees - all perhaps clones of a single seed with sub-soil interconnections. Most will have one leaf, but those with two (after up to seven years) produce a graceful, brown-streaked, yellow blossom resembling the open mouth of a hungry snake. The fish-shaped leaves display the speckled markings of a brook trout, and resemble the upright ears of a fawn. The yellow petals (sometimes white) of the nodding lily curve backwards on their leafless stems. The flower closes at night. Then all too soon the plant fades into the forest floor to await another year.

Edibility
Leaves and underground bulbs can be boiled and eaten. Flowers are edible – cooked or in a salad. The plant is high in nitrogen, easy to digest, and is sometimes over-grazed by rabbits and deer, although deer tend to eat only the flowers. Some say that the leaves have an apple flavor.

TROUT LILY

Erythronium americanum
Family: Lily
March – May

Native

Other Names
Dogtooth Violet
Adder's Tongue
Fawn Lily

Challenge
Observe the plant carefully. Which of the four common names seems most appropriate?
Estimate the ratio of flowers to leaves.

50 Wild Plants Everyone Should Know

ADDER'S TOUNGE

TROUT LILY

DOG TOOTH

Medicinal
Popular with Indians, they:

crushed and placed warm leaves over wounds.

prepared a root tea for fevers.

chewed raw leaves to prevent conception.

chewed on roots, then spit into water, to make fish bite.

Cancer treatment research has revealed chemicals that prevent genetic mutations.

Ecology
Flowers nourish queen bumblebees in early spring, and are pollinated by ants. The ants gather seeds and consume only the seed covering - distributing viable seeds over a large area.

DANDELION

Taraxacum officinale
Family: Composite
March - September

Alien

Other Names
Priests Crown
Wet-a-bed

Challenge
Legend: Blow once on seed-head. The remaining seeds are the number of children you will have.
Try nature's clock: the number of blows to remove all seeds is the hour of the day.
Watch the air-born seeds. They can fly for miles.

Description
Known as our most persistent lawn "weed", yet admired for its adaptability and significant medicinal qualities. An alien (at one time there were none in the U.S.), it escaped from the salad loving, colonists gardens and spread over the entire country. The many adaptations include: blossoms that produce over 100 parachuted seeds per flower, a deep tap-root that can grow even after cut into pieces, and a leaf structure that protects its space, and directs water to the root.

Explanation of the common names:

Dandelion – from French "Dent-De-Lion" - teeth of a lion, from the jagged, toothed leaves.

Wet-a-bed – stimulates the kidney and promotes urination

Priests Crown – from the flower which matures from yellow (golden-haired seminarian) to white headed pastor (seeds), to bald when seeds are gone (matured theologian).

Perhaps we would do well to reduce control by digging and poisoning, and learn to use dandelion and experience the benefits. Our mind-set should be that they are not just invading, worthless weeds - they have much to offer.

Edibility
It is grown commercially as a leaf vegetable. For a nutritious tea: steep one half ounce dried leaves in a cup for ten minutes.

The white leaf crowns at base of leaf are delicious raw or cooked. Use young leaves and buds in a salad or sandwich.

Cook leaves like spinach - boil until soft, replace water, re-boil.

Fry flowers like mushrooms.

"COFFEE" ROOTS

Nutritious "coffee" – wash summer or fall roots without removing brown covering, cut into pieces, roast until brown, crisp - grind. Pour small cupful into coffee pot, pour hot water - boil a few minutes. Dried cut roots will keep for years. Good before meals – promotes digestion.

Consumed by birds, pigs, goats, rabbits, but not sheep, horses or cattle.

Medicinal
Leaves are higher in vitamins A and C, and the minerals iron and potassium than spinach. A very effective diuretic, it reduces water weight (edema) and high blood pressure without causing mineral depletion. It controls acne, eczema, anemia, yeast infections, blood sugar, etc.

Very nourishing to the liver and gall bladder – stimulates bile production.

Try using the milky juice as a mosquito repellent and to remove warts and "age spots."

Ecology
Over 90 insects have been known to use this plant. Dandelion is an important source of nectar for honey bees.

The deep roots aid in breaking up hard soil. In the fall, a new rosette of leaves grows on top of the old leaf cluster, which promotes early spring growth. The flower is pollinated by insects, but can self-pollinate.

23 RAGWORT

Description
The bright, yellow flowers can quickly colonize an abandoned farm field, and turn it into a "sea of yellow." Growth is up to four feet tall. There is an average of twelve smooth, shiny, buttery petals (rays) on daisy-like, half inch flower heads. The lobed leaves appear as small torn rags (rag-wort). The octopus shaped roots are shallow and easy to pull.

Edibility
The foliage is considered poisonous to grazing animals. It contains toxic alkaloids which cause liver damage. Rabbits will nibble on young leaves.

Medicinal
Indians learned to use leaves and root tea for a variety of "female" disorders (Squaw-weed) and to relieve the pain of menstruation and childbirth.

Ecology
As a winter annual, seeds sprout in the fall and grow quickly after a spring rain. It prefers open, moist fields, but can be found in the woods, and has become much more common due to less herbicide use and "no-till" farming. Therefore growth is not disturbed by chemicals or plowing as in the past.

Bees and flies are attracted to the pollen and nectar. The seeds are covered by white hairs and are wind distributed.

RAGWORT

Senecio species
Family: Composite
April – July

Native

Other names
Butterweed
Cress-leaf squaw-weed

Challenge
Smell the "buttercup" aroma of the flower.

50 Wild Plants Everyone Should Know

YELLOW WOOD SORREL

Oxalis species
Family: Wood-Sorrel
May - October

Alien

Other Names
Sour Clover

Challenge
Chew on a leaf, flower or "little banana" seed capsule to detect the lemony flavor. Notice the middle leaf crease (where they fold) Are the leaves open or closed? If closed they are under some kind of stress (or in shade).

Description
Wood Sorrel has tiny, bright yellow flowers, with heart shaped, clover-like leaves that fold at night or when stressed. It will spread like a ground cover over poor soil, and can become a pesky weed in lawns and gardens. This may be the true shamrock – the national emblem of Ireland. St. Patrick used it to explain the Biblical Trinity to his audiences. The leaves were used as a model of the trinity, in paintings by Fra Angelica.

Edibility
Known as "hikers thirst quencher" – the entire lemon-flavored plant can be chewed. The leaves are used in salad and are high in vitamin C, phosphorus and potassium. However, it should be consumed sparingly. The sour taste is from oxalic acid found in many fruits and vegetables, which in large quantities can cause diarrhea, and bind to calcium.

Prepare wild lemonade by steeping a palm full of leaves in a pint of water, cool and sweeten.

Medicinal
The wild lemonade has a soothing affect on the digestive system – good for fever and sore throat. As a tea, it relieves fever, stomach cramps and nausea. Indians found if fed to horses, their running speed would increase..

Ecology
The flowers develop tiny, green, erect, banana shaped seed capsules, which when ripe, will burst open at the slightest touch, and catapult seeds as much as eight feet away. These tiny green "bananas" are a popular hikers' nibble.

50 Wild Plants Everyone Should Know

25 BIRD FOOT TREFOIL

BIRD FOOT TREFOIL

Lotus corniculatus
Family: Pea
May – September

Alien – from Europe

Other Names
Deer Vetch
Crow Toes

BIRD'S-FOOT SEED PODS

Description
By mid-June, bright yellow (rarely orange), pea-like flower clusters make their showy appearance in lawns and open fields along roadsides. They can become invasive – especially in lawns, and will compete for space with native plants using their sprawling foliage, and creeping root system. However, the attractive flower and the ability to grow on most any soil, has made it useful for erosion control as a ground cover, and even a grass substitute. Unusual for an alien, Trefoil is generally accepted, and has become useful in agriculture, and as a showy roadside plant.

There are five clover-like leaflets – the three middle ones much larger (tre-foil). The flowers produce seed-pods that resemble the toes of a birds foot (crow toes).

Edibility
The seed-pods are considered a trail-side nibble – but are small, and their resemblance to a bird's foot, tend to make them un-appetizing. The plant is high in protein, does not cause bloating, and is therefore valued as forage. Deer relish it.

Medicinal
The plant contains some poisonous cyanide, which in small quantities will stimulate respiration and digestion. Has been used in cancer treatment, but with caution due to the cyanide content.

Ecology
As a legume it fixes nitrogen, and enriches the soil. The abundant nectar has become important for bees.

Challenge
See if you can determine why the flowers are described as having a "powerful scent."
Look for the unusual birds-foot shaped seed-pods.

50 Wild Plants Everyone Should Know

WILD PARSNIP

Pastinaca sativa
Family: Parsnip
June – July

Alien – Europe

Other Names
Harts-eye

Challenge
When traveling, observe how common it is along roadsides. The tall, light yellow flower clusters are easy to identify.
Learn to distinguish it from a look-alike: Poison Hemlock which has white flowers and fern-like, dark green leaves. Parsnip leaflets are oval. Notice the abundance and variety of insects around the flower.

26 WILD PARSNIP

Description
Phyto-photo-dermatitus: probably never heard of by our pioneer forefathers who brought their treasured parsnip seeds to America to grow as a nourishing, starchy vegetable. The seeds produce a rosette of ground-hugging leaves, and a pale, carrot-like, fall-harvested root. Gradually, it was replaced by potatoes in early gardens. If the biennial parsnip roots are not harvested - the next spring they produce five-foot stems with clusters of umbrella-like tiny, pale yellow flowers, followed by hundreds of seeds. These parsnip hobos are making their way across the U.S. along roadways and open fields in ever-increasing numbers, and are causing serious human contact problems – often blamed on Poison Ivy.

The effect of skin contact with juice from broken stems and leaves is similar to Poison Ivy, causing blisters and burns, and made worse if skin is moist and then exposed to the sun after the contact. Producing more of a burn than an itch, phyto-photo-dermatitis (parsnip rash) can cause a dark skin discoloration for up to two years. Contact is usually made through efforts to eradicate, walking through a patch of the plants, or gathering the attractive flowers. The entire plant dies after seeds are produced at the end of the second year.

Edibility
First year parsnip roots (which have a rosette of leaves at ground level) can be gathered in the fall or early spring with a shovel. This is the same plant as the garden parsnip. The roots are up to 12" long and were relished in Europe. A hard frost sweetens the flavor. They can be used raw, but are usually cooked. Insects, including ladybugs, soldier beetles and wasps are constant visitors, seeking nectar and pollen. Cows avoid it, but deer graze on it and birds eat the seeds.

Irish beer was made by boiling the roots in water with hops.

Medicinal

While not scientifically verified, medieval folk used parsnips as an aphrodisiac.

If a rash develops from contact with the plant juices, medical treatment is advisable. It is important that the medical professional is aware of the cause (i.e. Parsnips and not Poison Ivy).

Ecology

Its rapid spread is due to:

1. Delayed roadside weed control after seed production.

2. No-till farming allowing it to become established in fields.

3. Abundant seeds, which remain viable for up to four years.

4. The ability to grow on disturbed soil (prefers a dry, sunny location).

MULLEIN

Verbascum Thapsus
Family: Snapdragon
June – September

Alien

Other Names
Flannel-leaf
Jacob's staff
Aaron's rod

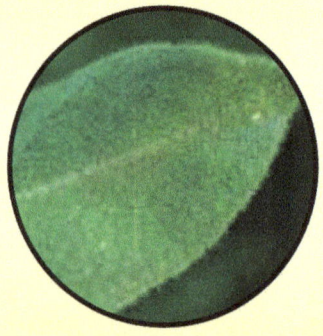

Challenge
Handle the leaves. They seem almost synthetic – soft, like velvet.
Check the flower stalk for insects and seed formation. The leaves sometimes have harmful insects called thrips, which appear as black specks.

Description
Few herbs have been held in such high regard, both for appearance, and effectiveness as a remedy for some of the most common health concerns of our forefathers. They brought it here from Europe and it has spread to all states.

As a biennial, the first year the seed produces a rosette of large ground level, thick leaves. They have a velvety covering of frosty, white hairs, which serve to conserve moisture and irritate the mouth of grazers. The leaves remain gray-green all winter and the next spring, an impressive flower stalk emerges growing up to eight feet tall in one summer. The tall flower stalks are commonly seen along roadsides and will grow in poor soil, and even gravel. The yellow flowers have a popcorn shape. The seeds (up to 200,000 per plant) will remain dormant in the soil for over 100 years.

Interesting uses include:
Seeds thrown into a pond will stun fish, making them easy to catch.

The stalks were used as funeral torches in Greece, and to light mines during the California gold rush.

May have been the biblical Aaron's rod – the "magic staff," used to overcome the sorcerers of Pharaoh.

Indians lined moccasins with the soft leaves for warmth.

Amish tobacco – dried leaves were allowed to be smoked, if used to relieve asthma.

Quaker's blush – girls (who were forbidden the use of cosmetics) managed a rosy complexion by rubbing leaves on their cheeks (nature's rouge).

Hunters' paper – used for emergency bathroom calls - also causes rosy "cheeks".

Flower tea, as a hair wash, turns hair a golden yellow.

FIRST-YEAR ROSETTE

Dried plants were kept in barns to repel mice.

Linked to witches – used to ward off evil spirits and curses.

Lover's faithfulness test - Girls would bend the stalk toward their home, and then periodically check to see if it stayed that way. If it did "he" was faithful. If the plant bent away, he was "wandering."

Dried seed stalks can make an attractive arrangement especially near fireplaces.

Edibility
Nourishing tea (first year leaves preferred):

Boil one teaspoon dried leaves in one cup of water 5 – 10 minutes. Strain through a coffee filter to remove hairs. Enjoy the soothing aroma and flavor.

Medicinal
Used as medicine for centuries, and backed by scientific evidence. Contains coumarin and hesperidin. Available in health stores.

Tea infusion: High in B vitamins - reduces stress. Has remarkable mild narcotic properties – pain killing and calms nerves. Relieves lung disorders, coughs, colds, asthma, upset stomach and diarrhea. May remove warts.

Oil (process flowers in a blender, cover with olive oil for two weeks – strain). Use as an antibiotic for ear ache, piles and bronchitis.

Ecology
The nectar attracts bees, but it can self-pollinate.

Has few natural enemies. Avoided by livestock and most insects.

Prefers bare soil. Other plants crowd it out.

50 Wild Plants Everyone Should Know

EVENING PRIMROSE

Oenothera biennis
Family: Evening Primrose
June – September

Native

Other Names
Sun Cups
Evening Star

Challenge
Look for the unusual cross-shaped stigma in the center of the flower.
Smell the flower and crushed leaves and try to determine the scent.

28 EVENING PRIMROSE

Description
Often seen along edges of fields, forests, and roadways with bright yellow, four petaled, fragrant blossoms. They are very sensitive to light intensity and the petals close in full sun. In the evening as the light dims- almost perceptibly, the petals respond and spread open releasing a sweet perfume, which attracts the pollinating Sphinx moth.

A biennial - first year leaf rosettes can be found in the spring at ground level among the old dried seedpod stalks. Dead stalks persist all winter, and with their woody seed-pods are attractive in dried plant arrangements. The beauty, edibility, and medicinal quality of primrose have resulted in world wide exportation.

Edibility
Entire plant is edible. Harvest leaves and roots in spring. Leaves are cooked like spinach.

First year roots (under spring rosettes) can be boiled to remove pungency, or French-fried. They have a parsnip flavor. The roots were relished by Indians. Flowers are used raw in salads.

Medicinal
Became well known and a popular supplement in the 1980s with the discovery that the seeds contained an oil rich in a valuable essential fatty acid: linolenic acid – which has significant health benefits, but is rare (it is in fish and flax) in most plants. It is beneficial for healthy skin, PMS symptoms, high blood pressure, arthritis, and M.S. The oil is extracted from seeds and capsules, and is sold in health stores. The seeds can be collected from dried pods (shake into a bag) and eaten raw for the health benefits.

Ecology
Seeds are a favorite of birds, especially goldfinches. Leaves attract Japanese beetles.

29 GOLDENROD

GOLDENROD

Family: Composite
Solidago sp
July – October

Native – now world wide

Other Names
Gold flower
Yellow Top

BALL GALL

Description
What do Thomas Edison, Henry Ford, and Goldenrod have in common?

Because of the rising cost of foreign tree latex, Edison searched for an alternative source of rubber. After testing thousands of plants at his lab in Ft. Myers, Florida, he chose goldenrod: it grows fast, is found all over the country, can be machine harvested, and contains a latex sap from which he was able to produce 12 pounds of rubber from 100 lbs. of leaves. By cross-breeding, he developed 12 foot plants (they are normally 2 – 3 feet tall). From his friend, Henry Ford, Edison received a Model T with tires made from goldenrod rubber. Edison turned his research over to the U.S. Government in the 1930's, but for now the goldenrod rubber is not cost competitive with petroleum rubber.

The bright yellow flower (which signals the end of summer) is becoming popular in ornamental gardens. It has been blamed for hay fever (rag weed - the real cause, blooms at the same time). Its pollen is too heavy to be carried by the wind. The pollen and nectar are important food sources for honey bees to survive the winter.

It is the state flower of Kentucky, Nebraska, and South Carolina. Some feel that it should be designated as our national flower.

Edibility
Flowers are an important source of nectar for honey. Pure goldenrod honey is light and spicy.

Tea – pour a cup of boiling water over two teaspoons of dried flowers or leaves. Steep for ten minutes and strain. Best to use Sweet Goldenrod (leaves without teeth when crushed have smell of anise)

The stem sap contains oil used as an ingredient in chewing gum, candles and deodorants.

Deer do not eat it.

Challenge
Identify the gall swelling by shape and location:
Ball gall – cut open and find fly maggot inside.
Elliptical gall – formed around moth eggs.
Bunch gall – from Midge fly - near top of stem, causing multiple flower branching.
Blister gall – looks like an ink spot on the leaf. Pull apart and find tiny larva inside.
See if you can find the sticky latex sap in the leaf veins of some plants. This was Edison's source of rubber.

Medicinal
The tea infusion is used for: colds, flu, fever, coughs, sore throat (Indians chewed the flowers) indigestion, lower back pain, arthritis, and high blood pressure.

Relieves kidney ailments – has aided in dissolving and passing kidney stones. As a diuretic, it flushes infected urinary systems. Drink plenty of water when using.

For kidney disease, should be used only under the direction of a professional.

Ecology
Abundant pollen and nectar attract many insects; especially wasps, bees, and butterflies. These, in turn, attract spiders and praying mantids.

Swellings along the stem are galls formed around eggs injected by insects.

Seems best suited to poor soil. In rich soil it grows up to eight feet and tends to fall over. One of the first plants to grow after a field has burned.

It is a perennial, and spreads from underground rhizomes into crowded colonies consisting of clones from a single plant.

MAROON, RED, PINK FLOWERS

Prairie Trillium / Toadshade

Ginger

Fire Pink

Wild Geranium

*Field Garlic, Wild Garlic, Wild Onion

Milkweed Common, Swamp, Butterfly Weed (orange)

*Red Clover

Joe-Pye Weed

*Alien

50 Wild Plants Everyone Should Know

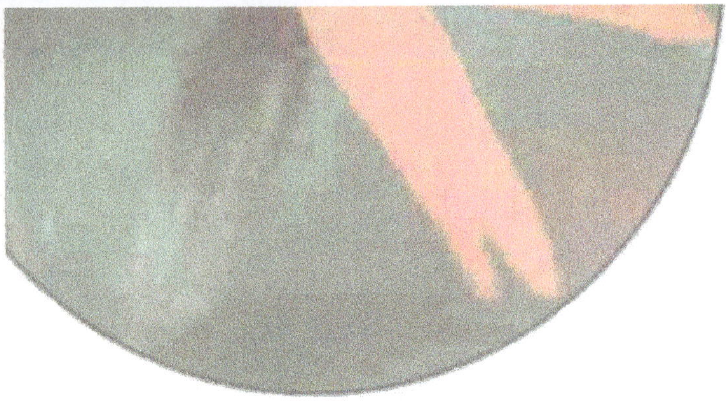

PRAIRIE TRILLIUM/TOADSHADE

PRAIRIE TRILLIUM/ TOADSHADE

Trillium recurvatum/ Trillium sessile
Family: Lily
April – May

Native

Other Names
Bloody Butcher

BIRTH ROOT

TOADSHADE

Description
Three claw-like maroon petals surround six purple stamens like a lampshade. Just below the flower are three camouflaged leaves speckled with patches of light and dark green. The flower may not be present, as the plant may need up to ten years to bloom. Finding a single specimen is unusual, as they spread into colonies from underground rhizomes.

Edibility
Young leaves are edible cooked or raw in a salad.

They are relished by deer.

Medicinal
Considered a sacred herb by Indians, the "birth" root tea was used to relieve cramps, promote menstruation and childbirth.

Raw root was grated and applied as a poultice to rheumatic joints.

Ecology
The name Prairie is perhaps a misnomer. Both will grow in full sun, but prefer woodlands. The flowers have no nectar, and are pollinated by bumblebees. The seeds are spread by ants.

Challenge
Smell the flower. Determine if there can be a scent without nectar.
Decide if the trillium you find is Prairie Trillium or Toadshade by the stems and sepals. The leaves and petals of Prairie narrow at the bottom into stalks. Sepals are under the leaves and point down. Toadshade has no apparent stalks, and the sepals are above the leaves.

50 Wild Plants Everyone Should Know

WILD GINGER

Asarum canadense
Family: Birthwort
April – May

Native

Other Names
Cat-foot
Colic Root

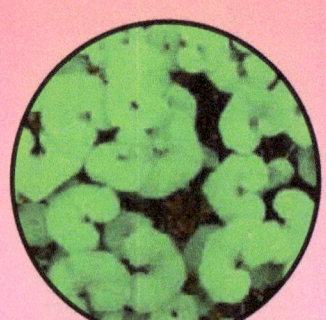

GINGER ROOT

**Challenge
(only if abundant)**
Break open a stem and/or a piece of the shallow, horizontal root stock. Crush and smell to detect the ginger-like odor.

31 WILD GINGER

Description
Ginger is usually encountered in the woods as a dense blanket of green, heart-shaped leaves with no apparent flowers. Close inspection reveals, at the ground level junction of each pair of leaves, an attractive maroon bloom about one inch across. The leaves rise from creeping stems that spread in all directions, resulting in a thick ground cover. The flowers smell like a dead animal. Meskwaki Indians chewed on the stem then spit on bait to improve chances of catching fish. The leaves remain green all winter.

Edibility
Our native ginger is not related to the popular flavoring ginger from the tropics, but has a similar taste, and can be used as a substitute. Hard candy has been made from the stem juice. Native Americans used it to sanitize and flavor meat and fish.

Medicinal
The stem juice was very popular with the Indians as a treatment for whooping cough, indigestion, fever, and sore throat.

Ginger contains an anti-tumor compound called aristolochic acid, and is a very effective herbal for relieving nausea and air/riding sickness. It is available in capsule form. It has become less common in the wild, and is protected in some states.

Ecology
The foul smelling flower attracts insects, which help in pollination. It seems to thrive in the shade.

FIRE PINK

Silene virginica
Family: Pink
April – June

Native

Other Names
Catchfly
Indian Pink

Challenge
Look for a "claw" at the base of the petals, and at the top of the tube.
Find seed capsules with kidney shaped seeds. They form while the plant is still blooming.

Description
Encountering a patch of Fire Pink in the woods – even from a distance, can be startling. The pure red, five-petaled pinwheels are perhaps the most brilliant color in nature.

On the outer ends of the petals are pink tinged notches. At the base of the petals is a tiny, hairy "claw." The beauty and popularity of Fire Pink was expressed in 1997 when 27,000 Indiana 4th graders voted to promote it to become the state flower. (Currently the Indiana state flower is peony, which is from China) The "Flower Bill" was sponsored, but was not granted a hearing.

Edibility / Medicinal
It is not edible and the Indians considered the plant poisonous. They perceived that the bright red color was a warning sign.

Ecology
The stem grows up to twenty inches both erect and prostrate on the ground. It prefers rocky slopes in semi-shade. A similar species, called Royal catch-fly, has sticky hairs on the stem and a flower that traps insects. Fire Pink is pollinated by the ruby-throated hummingbird, which is attracted to the red color and sugary nectar in the long tubes at the base of the flower. The nectar is difficult for insects to reach.

It is endangered in some states, including Wisconsin and Florida.

WILD GERANIUM

Geranium maculatum
Family: Geranium
April – June

Native

Other Names
Cranesbill

Challenge
Look for the nectar guides- fine lines in petals that direct insects to the nectar glands.
If in seed stage, try to activate the explosive seed-pods by carefully touching them.

Description
While not related to the common red garden geranium (from South Africa), the native geranium has its own unique beauty. Color hues range through rose, lavender, soft pink, light blue, to purple. The striking flowers are becoming popular in flower gardens. A perennial, it spreads into colonies by underground rhizomes. The open seed-pods resemble little brown flowers with curled petals. The flowers are a favorite of butterflies and moths. The leaves and rhizomes contain brown tannin which the pioneers used for tanning hides.

Edibility
Deer graze on the foliage

Chipmunks consume the seeds

Medicinal / Nutritional
A tea infusion is made from the entire plant or roots alone. It was used, especially by Indians, as a mouthwash or gargle to treat sore throat, tooth-ache, thrush, and canker sores. Extracted geranium oil is still used in skin care products and to help control acne. Pioneers learned to use the root for diarrhea, and injected it to "strengthen weak rectal and vaginal muscles."

Ecology
As the seed capsules mature into a one-inch "cranes bill," a tension develops, which causes the capsule to spring open and fling seeds up to 30 feet. This can be activated by simply touching the mature brown pods. Upon landing, the seed "creeps" into the ground by moving its "tail."

34 WILD GARLIC, FIELD GARLIC, WILD ONION

FIELD GARLIC FLOWERS

Description
There are many species of *Allium*. They grow in fields and woodlands and resemble clumps of tall grass. The three most likely encountered are described.

Field Garlic, *Allium vineale* - alien - from Europe and Asia. Flowers May – July

Leaves – round, hollow, waxy, with a strong garlic scent.

Bulb – covered with a brown sheath

Flowers – pink, green, or white. Sometimes there are tiny bulb clusters with tails.

Wild Garlic, *Allium canadense* - native, flowers May – July

Leaves – flat, grass-like with an onion scent

Bulb – covered by tan fibers

Flowers – pink, white, with tiny reddish bulbs

Wild Onion, *Allium stellatum* - native, flowers July - August

Leaves – flat, grass-like, onion scent

Bulb – covered with brown sheath

Flowers – reddish pink or white, usually in a round cluster with many tiny bulbs

FIELD GARLIC, WILD GARLIC, WILD ONION

Allium sp.
Family: Lily
May – August

Alien, Native, Native

Challenge
Crush and smell the leaves. Only the alien, hollow-leaved Field Garlic smells like garlic. Wild Garlic and Wild Onion have an onion odor.
Carefully pull on the leaf at the base to bring up the bulb.

50 Wild Plants Everyone Should Know

WILD GARLIC

WILD ONION

Edibility
Leaves and bulbs are edible raw or cooked, and have a strong flavor. Chop young leaves into a salad to enhance the flavor and provide a health boost. The bulbs may be too strong if used raw. If consumed by cattle, the plants impart a garlic flavor to milk, or if harvested with wheat, garlic flavored flour can result. It is a favorite of wild turkey and ground squirrels.

Medicinal / Nutritional
Garlic has a long, impressive history as a safe, beneficial herb for a variety of health concerns, including high cholesterol and blood pressure, TB, parasites, acne, bacterial infections, colds, bronchitis, diabetes, poor digestion, energy enhancer, and insect repellent.

Ecology
The tiny bulblets (up to 300) from the flower drop to the ground and take root. These plants can become numerous and invasive (especially the alien Field Garlic) and spread into lawns and pastures. They are resistant to herbicides.

35 MILKWEED

COMMON MILKWEED

MILKWEED

Asclepias sp
Family: Milkweed
May – September

Native

Other Names
Silkweed
Rabbit Milk
Indian hemp

SWAMP MILKWEED

"MILK" FROM CUT STEM

Description
There are three Milkweed species most likely encountered:

Common - *A. syriaca*
Flowers - dull rose, purplish; up to six feet tall; white sticky stem juice

Swamp – *A. incarnata*
Flowers – deep pink; up to four feet tall; thin, white stem

Butterfly Weed – *A. tuberosa*
Flowers – orange; up to two and one half feet tall; stem juice clear and watery.

Perhaps best known for its relationship to the monarch butterfly, Common Milkweed is the only food of the orange and black monarch larvae. They feed on the stem and leaves, and absorb the milky juice which is passed on to the adult Monarch. Birds, attracted to the Monarch for food, find them distasteful and toxic, and will actually vomit if they swallow a Monarch. Birds seem to learn from their first experience, and have been observed cautiously nibbling on butterfly wings as if testing their edibility.

Edibility
Myths abound regarding the edibility of milkweed, which is unfortunate because it is common, tasty, and easy to harvest.

There are reports of the milky sap of Common Milkweed being bitter and even poisonous. However, there are wild food experts who disagree, and commonly use young shoots, flower buds, and young pods for food.

Shoots (found in May) are as long as 14" and should be cooked for up to 20 minutes.
Flower buds (found in July and August) can be boiled or steamed.
Young pods (August – Sept.) Make an excellent cooked, green vegetable.

Pour off water used for cooking. It should not be necessary to change water several times as some suggest.

Challenge
Try to remove the thin fibers from the stems. Indians used these for sewing thread and fishing lines. Smell the flowers. The fragrance has been described as "overwhelming".

MONARCH ON SWAMP MILKWEED

BUTTERFLY WEED

BUTTERFLY WEED

POD RELEASING SEEDS

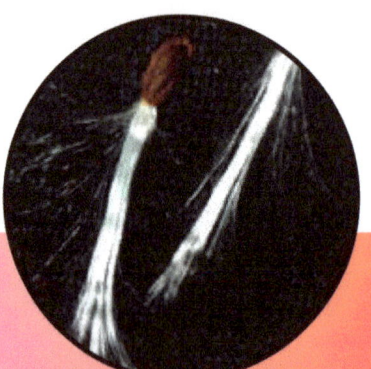
SEEDS WITH SILK

Medicinal / Nutritional

Studies have suggested that cardiac glycosides in the juice may be useful in treating heart disease. However, if consumed, Common Milkweed juice may cause hot flashes and rapid heart rate.

Covering warts with the white sap may remove them. Apply every day for two to three weeks.

Indians used root tea for lung ailments. Mixed one to one with water, the sap can relieve sunburn and poison ivy.

Ecology

Insects and hummingbirds are attracted to the abundant, fragrant nectar.

Insects get trapped by the sticky juice, which is in all parts of the plant.

Plants grow well along roadsides (Common), dry fields (Butterfly Weed), and wet soil (Swamp).

Chiggers have been associated with milkweed.

The large seed-pods burst open suddenly in the fall, releasing hundreds of parachuted seeds. Goldfinches use the "parachutes" to line their nests.

Baltimore Orioles use stem fibers to weave their hanging nests.

Challenge

Open a warty, football shaped seed pod. Release the seeds and watch them blow in the wind like miniature parachutes. Notice the silky texture of the seeds. They can be used to stuff pillows, mattresses and sleeping bags in place of feathers. Hold them under water – they will not get wet. They were used in World War I flight suits. If a pilot crashed into water, he would float.

36 RED CLOVER

Description
Red Clover arrived in the U.S. along with the British colonists primarily as a valued livestock and poultry food. The familiar rose to pink, globe-shaped flower heads are made up of clusters of 20 – 100 individual florets. The three green leaflets, which became a model for the clubs on playing cards, are two toned green with a light green V shape in the middle. The three parted leaves resembled the design of the great three parted club carried by the warrior, Hercules.

The association with Ireland is from the legend that St. Patrick used it to explain the Holy Trinity. So impressed were the Irish that since the 1600's they began wearing the three leaves on their hats on St. Patrick's Day - March 17. However, yellow wood sorrel may be the original shamrock.

It has been designated as the state flower of Vermont. Finding the rare four-leaf clover continues to be a sign of good luck.

Edibility
Makes a tasty, healthy tea. Pour a pint of boiling water over one tablespoon dried or fresh flowers - steep twenty minutes and strain. Young leaves are used in salad or cooked as a vegetable.

Medicinal / Nutritional
It is a blood purifier and improves dry skin. The plant contains calcium, magnesium, phosphorus, potassium, sodium, chromium, thiamin, folic acid, niacin, and vitamin C.

Cancer treatment - Research continues on at least four tumor-inhibiting compounds found in the plant. As a fertility aid - its high folic acid promotes sperm and egg production. There are isoflavones which have an estrogen-like affect that aids in controlling osteoporosis. The tea relieves a dry, spasmodic cough.

Heart disease – lowers LDL by increasing bile production. It is a blood thinner, and tones arteries.

Used in skin creams and for controlling psoriasis.

Ecology
The roots have bacterial nodules, which absorb nitrogen and enrich the soil, and are therefore useful in crop rotation. The flowers are an important source of nectar for the production of high quality honey. It readily adapts to disturbed soil, and If crowded will grow upright, or sprawl along the ground, forming large clumps.

RED CLOVER

Trifolium pretense
Family: Pea
May – September

Alien

Other Names
Cow Grass
Shamrock
Purple Clover

Challenge
Carefully remove a single purple floret. Suck on the bottom for a taste of the sweet nectar.

JOE-PYE-WEED

Eupatorium purpureum/ maculatum/fistulosum
Family: Composite
July – September

Native

Other Names
Queen-of-the-Meadow
Gravel Root

Challenge
From the description under Other Names, try to distinguish among Sweet, Spotted and Hollow Joe-pye-weed.
Crush a leaf and smell the apple-like odor.

Description
Three Main Species:

E. purpureum, Sweet Joe-pye-weed. Green stem with whorls of three or four leaves. Crushed leaves have an apple or vanilla smell.

E. maculatum, Spotted Joe-pye-weed. Purple or purple spotted stem, whorls of four or five leaves.

E fistulosum, Hollow Joe-pye-weed. Light purple hollow stem, which depresses if pinched. Whorls of six leaves.

Named after Joe Pye – a friendly, native Mohegan Indian from Connecticut. He taught early settlers in the 1700's how to use this plant to cure the dreaded typhoid fever.

It has a regal appearance (Queen-of-the-Meadow) and towers over other plants with a height of up to twelve feet. The large domed, fuzzy flower clusters range in color from white to shades of purple, pink and rose. It is attractive enough to be used in flower gardens and privacy borders. The flowers turn into fluffy white seed heads.

Edibility
A delicate, medicinal tea is made by pouring a cup of boiling water over a teaspoon of dried flowers and steeping for ten minutes.

Leaves are consumed by rabbits and deer.
Seeds are eaten by mice, mallards, and turkeys.
The flowers, with abundant nectar, are like magnets to bees and butterflies.

Medicinal / Nutritional

An extract of the root is prepared by briefly boiling three ounces of root in three pints of water. A ritual of drinking three cups a day was used by Indians, and still is in Appalachia, for treating kidney disorders, constipation, poor circulation, menstrual cramps, and gout. The Chippewa rubbed leaves on restless children to induce sleep.

Meskwaki Indians considered it an aphrodisiac: "a love medicine to be nibbled while speaking to women when they are in a wooing mood."

Ecology

A perennial, it forms colonies, spreading from rhizomes.

The long pistils become "hairs" that transport the seeds by wind. It prefers moist soil, and will stabilize loose marsh soil.

PURPLE, VIOLET FLOWERS

Thistle-Field, Bull*, Canada*

Ironweed

*Alien

50 Wild Plants Everyone Should Know

THISTLE

(Many species)
Family: Composite
July – October

Native and alien

FIELD THISTLE

BULL THISTLE LEAVES

Description
Alien thistles have been declared: "the worst weed in the entire U.S."

They grow up to nine feet tall and the alien species spread rapidly, crowding out native plants. The native Field thistle, *Cirsium discolor* is not so aggressive. The leaves are covered with very sharp spines. "If you get close, you get poked." The large pink, lavender, or purple flowers are fragrant and attractive. It is hard to find a flower not covered by an assortment of insects. Goldfinches love thistles, and delay nesting until late summer, waiting for the seeds with the soft thistledown. The Painted Lady butterfly uses thistle for its entire life cycle.

Edibility
Young leaves with spines removed are excellent in salads. First year roots are edible, raw or cooked – similar to carrots.

Challenge
Try to identify the three most common thistles: Field thistle: (native) large, one to two inch pale, purple flowers, no spines on stem. Undersides of leaves have fine hairs like white wool. Bull thistle: (Alien – from Eurasia) large one to two inch rose-purple flower, very spiny; prickly wings on stem. Canada thistle (Alien – came to U.S. from Europe through Canada) Three-fourths inch pale lilac flower on many branches. No spines on stem. May be our most common thistle.

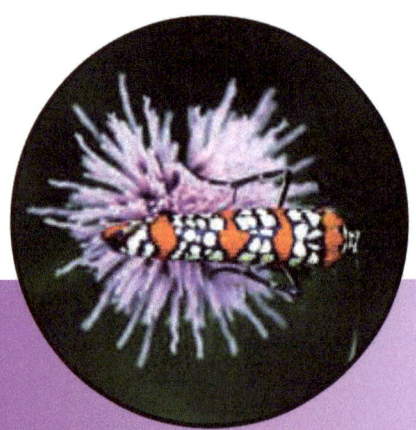
CANADA THISTLE

CANADA THISTLE

Medicinal / Nutritional

Blessed Milk Thistle, *Carduus marianus*, from Europe, has been very popular for thousands of years for a variety of liver problems, including cirrhosis and jaundice. Scientific research continues to evaluate its effectiveness, including the reduction of insulin resistance and inhibition of cancer cells. The active component is silymarin, extracted from ripe seeds. Health stores carry thistle products. Milk thistle has pale green leaves with white veins. There is a cluster of spiny leaves at the base of the purple flowers. The stem is not spiny.

Ecology

The seeds have a cluster of small bristles, and are wind carried, sometimes for miles. However, the seeds are heavy and most tend to fall to the ground. Some thistles spread rapidly from underground stems. Most are biennials. They have few natural enemies. The spines are an effective deterrent to grazing animals. They are excellent butterfly plants.

IRONWEED

Vernonia altissima/gigantean
Family: Composite
August – October

Native

Other Names:
Several species including: New York, Tall, and Western Ironweed

SEEDS

Description
About the time many summer flowers are fading, ironweed produces rich, reddish-purple blooms like crimson torches, at the top of tall stems. The name refers to the tough stems that grow up to ten feet, yet can resist strong wind. Stems have been used for stakes and kite building. Flowers are attractive enough to be used in home landscaping and in cut flower arrangements.

Edibility
The flowers are an important nectar source for bees and butterflies. The plant can become a troublesome weed – spreading across over-grazed pastures. Leaves are bitter and are avoided by cattle. If cattle do consume them, they may contact a leaf rust fungus which has been linked to abortion.

Medicinal / Nutritional
American Indians learned to use the leaves and roots to prepare a tea which they used as a "blood tonic" to treat stomach aches, menstruation, and childbirth pain.

Ecology
As a tall perennial and prolific seed producer, ironweed spreads rapidly in fields where there is little competition.

Challenge
Try to break the stem to experience its strength. Smell the flower to determine if there is any aroma. Most people detect no scent.

BLUE FLOWERS

Violet

Blue Phlox

*Chicory

Great Lobelia

*Alien

COMMON BLUE VIOLET

COMMON BLUE VIOLET

Viola species
Family: Violet
March – June

Native

Other Names
Johnny Jump Ups
Chicken Fights
Rooster Heads
The "cool" name is vy-O-la.

Description
Color ranges from pure white to deep purple, blue and yellow. Only white has an aroma - like vanilla. It is a symbol of love and faithfulness. This was Napoleons favorite flower, and he was often seen with it pinned to his clothing. It can be an attractive ground cover, and will invade a lawn that has acidic soil.

Pansies were developed from Wild Violet. It is the state flower of Rhode Island, New Jersey, Illinois and Wisconsin – where it was chosen by a vote of school children in 1908.

Edibility
Young flowers and leaves make a good trail-side nibble or tea. They are high in vitamins A and C. Young leaves are used like spinach. They have a unique taste: mild, sweet, peppery. Yellow flowers may have a laxative effect!

Make candied violet flowers by dipping them in boiling sugar syrup and air dry. Violet jelly was a pioneer favorite. The plant is not harmed by picking the colorful flowers since they don't produce seeds. The seeds develop in tiny flowers under the leaves later in the season.

Challenge
Examine the five petals: two upper, two on the sides with little white beards, one lower with veins that serve as a landing pad for insects. You may find a hook or spur below the petal, used for a pioneer game similar to breaking a chicken wishbone (reason plant is called Chicken Fights or Rooster-heads). Two people find flowers with a hook – hook them together and pull until a flower comes off. The winner's wish may come true.

NORTHERN WHITE VIOLET

SWEET WHITE VIOLET

DOWNY YELLOW VIOLET

Medicinal / Nutritional

Leaf tea is a blood purifier. It is very high in Vitamin C and salicylic acid (aspirin), and treats colds, coughs, headaches, and lung congestion. The leaves also contain rutin, which is good for varicose veins and strengthening capillaries.

Ecology

Flowers are high in nectar, but not often visited by insects. Tiny brown flowers form capsules later in the season that fling seeds three to four feet. Leaves are eaten by deer and rabbits.

BLUE PHLOX

BLUE PHLOX

Phlox divaricata
Family: Phlox
April – June

Native

Other Names
Sweet William

Description
Discovering a blooming colony of Blue Phlox in early spring provides a spectacular sight. They almost appear as a misplaced flower garden in the forest. The delicate blue blooms cluster on fifteen-inch stems. The flowers are fragrant, and provide early spring nectar for hummingbirds and butterflies- especially the tiger swallowtail.

Edibility / Medicinal
While leaf tea has been used as a blood purifier, and to treat eczema, the beauty of Phlox supersedes their limited edibility and medicinal qualities.

Ecology
They are available in nurseries and are very popular in rock gardens, and as a ground cover under trees. They are perennial and form colonies by leafy shoots that spread along the ground, rooting at the nodes.

They are often called Sweet William. However, Sweet William, *Phlox maculata*, blooms later in the summer, is taller – up to three feet, tends to be pink, and has purple spotted stems. Both prefer moist soil and are found along streams.

Challenge
Try to find the small, green seed-pods. When ripe, they will explode to release the seeds.
Smell the flowers. The fragrance is "unforgettable".
Check the stems. Notice that they are both hairy and sticky.

CHICORY

Cichorium intybus
Family: Composite
June – October

Alien – imported by colonists from Europe

Other Names
Ragged Sailor
Coffee Weed

"COFFEE" ROOT

Challenge
Look for the rare albino flower.
Place cut flowers in water. The blue will fade quickly to white.
Try to pull up or dig out the long, white tap-root to observe the coffee substitute.

42 CHICORY

Description
The light blue flowers brighten its favorite habitat: roadsides, where clusters can be viewed for miles at a time. On a sunny day, the flower opens very early, and then closes by mid-day, never to open again.

It is best known for the long, tan root, used as a coffee additive or substitute. During World War II, most U.S. coffee was made from cultivated chicory root. It has no caffeine, and is regaining popularity, especially in the South, including New Orleans. This European alien received high-level recognition in the U.S. as a favorite of Thomas Jefferson and George Washington.

Edibility
To prepare the root; peel, then roast at 250 degrees up to four hours, until dark brown and fragrant. Grind and brew until strong and dark - add honey. The root is tough, but edible raw - chop into a salad or steam.

Young leaves are used as a salad green. They are slightly bitter, but very nutritious. Under cultivation it is grown in darkness to keep leaves tender. Endive and radicchio are derived from chicory.

It is considered a valuable fresh food for grazing animals and rabbits.

Medicinal / Nutritional
To produce a diuretic, laxative and to lower blood sugar – heat one ounce of root in one pint water. Young boiled roots treat jaundice, constipation, and an evil disposition!

Ecology
Seems to prefer poor, wet soil. Can become invasive, and will out-compete native plants.

43 GREAT LOBELIA

GREAT LOBELIA

Lobelia siphilitica
Family: Bluebell
August – September

Native

Other Names
Blue Cardinal Flower

Challenge
Look for the pistil hanging above the flower opening, which bees contact, and pollinate as they enter the flower for nectar.

Description
Visualize lobelia as a face with only a mouth. The upper lip has two ear-like lobes. The lower lip has three lobes, which serve as a landing for bumble bees, where they can enter the mouth in search of nectar. The throat has attractive blue and white stripes. The sky-blue and white flower clusters emerge in late summer, and have become popular in wildflower gardens. Stems grow up to four feet tall.

Edibility
The plant is considered poisonous to eat, and no parts should be ingested. However, Meskwaki Indians determined that the root was a love potion, and would secretly place finely ground root powder in the food of an arguing couple. Too much caused vomiting. (And at least delayed the disagreement)

Most animals, except deer, avoid it.

Medicinal / Nutritional
It was well-known as a secret Indian remedy for syphilis (see species name) and roots were sold to Europeans. However, effectiveness has been scientifically disputed.

Indians used a leaf tea to treat colds, fevers, and coughs. They inhaled flowers for a stuffy nose.

This is not the same lobelia that is used by herbalists for respiratory disorders. That lobelia is known as Indian tobacco, *l. inflata*. It has a small pale-violet flower.

Ecology
Lobelia likes wet feet (soil) and is found growing in low areas, along streams. It sometimes hybridizes with the red cardinal flower, producing a deep red flower. It is a perennial, but lives only two to three years, and relies on bumblebees for pollination.

GREEN FLOWERS

Jack-in-the-Pulpit

Horsetail (no flowers – has green or brown cones)

Poison Ivy

Cattail

Solomon's Seal

*Stinging Nettle

Ragweed, Common and Giant

*Alien

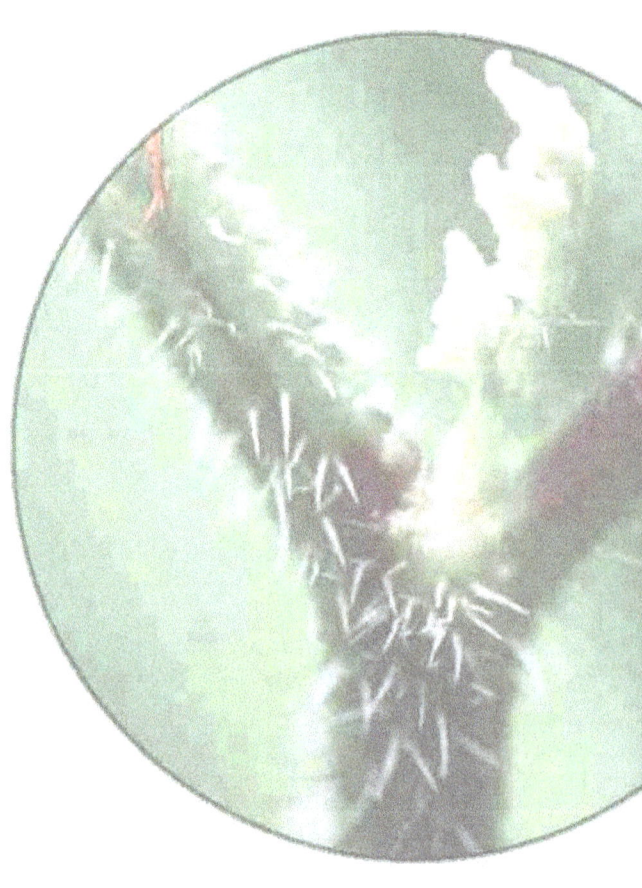

JACK-IN-THE-PULPIT
44

JACK-IN-THE-PULPIT

Arisaema triphyllum
Family: Arum
April – June

Native

Other Names
Indian turnip
Wake Robin

JILL TWO JACKS

INDIAN "TURNIP"

Description

You may need to crouch down to see "Pastor Jack" peeking from his striped overhead pulpit canopy. The flower spikes we call Jack are "multi-racial: he can be black, white, brown, green or striped. Jack himself is the upper part of the flower. The tiny reproductive parts are at the base of the spike we call Jack. The canopy covering Jack varies from light green to green with dark stripes.

Amazingly, Jack can become a Jill. If growing conditions are favorable, and enough energy is stored, Jack will grow larger, produce two sets of compound leaves, and become a Jill, with female flower parts. If weather conditions become unfavorable - next year, Jill will produce only one leaf and become a Jack again with male flower parts. Therefore, large plants, with two leaf stalks, are Jills. Small plants with one leaf stalk are Jacks. To verify, examine the base of the spike – female flower parts (pistils) look like tiny green berries. These will produce seeds with toxic, bright red berry clusters in the fall. Male flowers (stamens) look like tiny threads. Single specimens have been found that contain both pistils and stamens, and are called Jack and Jill.

Challenge

Lightly squeeze "Jack," and rotate back and forth. The squeak is Jack "preaching." Try to determine if the plant is a Jack or a Jill.

GREEN BERRIES   **RIPE BERRIES**   **FEMALE MALE**

Edibility

The root (tuber) up to two inches in width is called Indian turnip. It contains calcium oxalate crystals. If chewed- after a short time, there is intense burning in the mouth. Indians avoided this by drying, or boiling three times before eating it as a vegetable. Raw, it can cause throat swelling and suffocation. The Meskwakis placed chopped raw root into meat, and laid it out for their Sioux enemies who then became sick or died from oxalate poisoning. When dried, roasted, or boiled the root develops a chocolate flavor.

In some Indian tribes, young men were required to consume one raw root to enter manhood.

Grazing animals can be poisoned by consuming the entire plant.

The red berries are poisonous to humans, but attract many wild animals.

Medicinal / Nutritional

Pawnees powdered the root and applied to temples for headaches.

Indians mixed a teaspoon of dried root in cold water as a short term contraceptive —using too much caused sterility.

Ecology

The plant is becoming rare in some areas. However, it is easily grown from seed.

BRANCHED FORM

HORSETAIL

Equisetum arvense / hyemale
Family: Horsetail
April – October

Native

Other names
Scouring Rush
Bottlebrush
Dinosaur grass

MATURE CONE

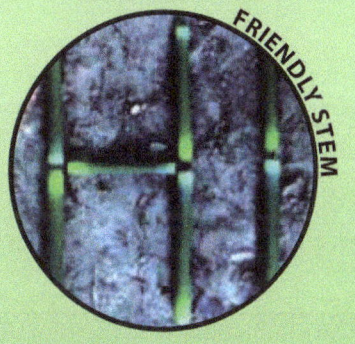

FRIENDLY STEM

Description
Horsetails are miniaturized survivors of the Age of Dinosaurs. Fossil records show that they dominated the landscape 400 million years ago in giant forests, and grew up to 90 feet tall. Dinosaurs roamed these forests and grazed on the young plants and tender branch-lets. Today, environmental changes have reduced their size (but not their shape) to two - five feet tall.

They have no flowers, seeds, or true leaves. There are two main types: *E. arvens* has whorls of branch-lets that give it the appearance of a green horse's tail. They have been tied to work horse's tails as an extension, to ward off flies. *E. hyemale* is a single bamboo - like jointed stem that resembles asparagus, and has no branches. Both grow in crowded colonies. At the top of some of the stems, cones form, that release reproductive spores (like ferns). Like a natural form of Lego or pop beads, the hollow, jointed stems can be pulled apart, then, re-joined if placed in the original order.

The stems absorb silica (sand) from the soil, giving them a rough, gritty texture. Pioneers used them like brillo pads to scour pots and pans. Indians used them like a file to sharpen their arrowheads. With practice, they can be used as sand paper to give a fine satin finish to wood or metal. They have been used to sand the reeds on clarinet and saxophones. Gold has been found in the stem tissue, but not enough to warrant extraction.

Edibility
Young shoots are edible in small amounts - boiled or pickled. However, if livestock graze on it, a serious thiamine (B vitamin) deficiency can result. Indians found that when fed in restricted amounts, horsetail helped their geese and ponies gain weight.

Challenge
When encountered, imagine these plants 90 feet tall, and one foot in diameter.
Try to find the grenade shaped spore producing cones at the top of some of the stems.
Pull a stem apart at the joints (they are tight) and try to put them back together like pop beads.
Try using as sandpaper to smooth a piece of wood, or to shine a penny.

STEMS WITHOUT BRANCHES

Medicinal

Horsetail continues to be an effective, medicinal herb, used to treat skin, hair, nails, arthritis, ulcers, eczema, bladder, kidney, prostate, etc. Its effectiveness is due to its high mineral content. Silica helps the body absorb calcium. It heals cartilage and reduces inflammation, and seems to function as an internal cosmetic. There is an isolated report of a lady who claims to have healed herself of terminal cancer by drinking five cups of horsetail tea daily.

Ecology

Horsetail prefers wet, sandy soil, and is often found along river-banks and in shallow water. It spreads by underground rhizomes, and can form dense colonies which can become invasive, and once established, becomes a persistent perennial. It provides a favorite landing site for dragonflies.

Horsetail has been used as a fungicide on domestic plants. Mix one and a half ounces of dried stems in one gallon of water. Boil 20 minutes. Strain and cool. Spray on infected plants.

POISON IVY

Toxicodendron radicans
Family: Cashew
May – June

Native

Other Names
Markweed

Description
"Leaflets of three let it be." Good advice – Poison Ivy with its three leaf clusters contain an oil-urushiol, so toxic that an amount the size of the head of a pin could affect up to 500 people. Young spring leaves are dark red, then turn green in summer and reddish - orange in fall. The tiny flowers are green and yellow. They produce green berries that turn cream colored. It grows as ground cover, a vine - climbing high into trees, and as a shrub or a small tree with a four inch diameter stem. Claims are made that just walking near it can cause an allergic reaction. However, contact must be made with the oil, which can be carried in smoke, on animal hair, or clothing. The oil will remain active as long as five years. Indian warriors were the first to use poison gas warfare: they made down- wind bonfires of poison ivy exposing their enemies to infected smoke.

There is evidence that we are born with natural immunity, but become sensitized with repeated exposure, so that adults are more likely to get it than kids. The poison is in resin canals throughout the plant. It is possible to touch an undamaged leaf and not become infected, but leaves are usually broken or chewed by an insect, and the oil has leaked out. The similar Poison Oak prefers warm climates, and extends from New Jersey south to Florida, then west through Texas and California. The leaves are leathery, hairy, and oak-like, and tend to grow as a shrub.

Edibility
Birds are fond of the fruits, and distribute seeds through droppings. Goats eat the leaves, and the claim has been made that drinking their milk will impart immunity. The late naturalist Euell Gibbons, gained immunity by consuming three tiny leaflets, then larger leaves the next day, etc. until he ate three full size leaves. This is not recommended, as dangerous internal reaction could result.

Challenge
Notice that the leaf margins have coarse teeth and the middle leaf has a longer stem than the two side leaves. Look for the five leaflet Virginia Creeper which grows as a vine and appears similar to poison Ivy on tree trunks.

POISON IVY VA. CREEPER

Medicinal

Wash exposed areas thoroughly with cold water and oil - less soap (detergent) within an hour. The itchy water blisters are not contagious, and scratching will not spread it, but may cause infection. Effective drug store remedies are constantly being developed. Serious cases are controlled with steroids.

You cannot get Poison Ivy from other people unless the invisible urushiol resin is still on their skin or clothing.

Natural remedies such as Jewelweed and Plantain are often growing near poison Ivy. Rubbing stem juice from these plants over the infected area can prevent the itchy rash. Lemon juice or an ice cube can be soothing.

A homeopathic tincture, made of poison ivy, known as Rhus tox, is used to treat eczema, arthritis, sprains, virus infections, and heavy menstruation.

Ecological

The rapid growth and leaf density provide animal cover and erosion control. All parts of the plant are toxic, and infections can be contracted year around. It is especially infectious at night or in shade. No animals are known to become infected.

CATTAIL

Typha latifolia
Family: Cattail
May – July

Native

Other names
Candlestick
Water Torch
Flax tail

Description
The familiar brown, cigar shaped spike is the female flower composed of compacted hairs attached to over 200,000 tiny seeds. In the spring the young flower is green, and is composed of two parts: the pollen producing male (at the top of the flower) and the future brown female. After producing abundant pollen, which falls on the female, the male shrivels into a dry twig, withers away, and by late spring falls off. The female turns brown and plump as it produces seeds, and ends up looking like a roasted wiener on a stick. By fall, it can grow up to nine feet tall. The brown flower spike turns furry and white as it breaks apart and releases the wind driven seeds. The flower head can be dipped in oil and used as a torch. Indians learned to weave the long flat leaves into baskets, floor mats, and wigwam covers. The soft, downy seeds were used as a stuffing in pillows and sleeping bags.

Edibility
As a food source, cattail is tasty and nutritious, but requires skill and effort to harvest.

In the spring, the soft flower shoots are enclosed in a leafy sheath. They are boiled and eaten like asparagus or corn-on-the-cob. The bases of young leaves are white and eaten like artichokes.

Pollen can be collected by tying bags around the flowers in the spring. The pollen is mixed with whole grain flour to make pancakes and corn bread, or sprinkled over a salad. The soft white, starchy tips of underwater roots and rhizomes can be peeled and boiled.

The leaves and seeds are inedible, and may be poisonous to livestock.

Challenge
In the spring, try to find the edible flower shoots, growing among the leaves and covered with a leaf sheath.
Remove all the seeds and imagine using the rough flower stem as a toothbrush – which the Indians did.
Collect some firm brown flower spikes and place them in a vase to make an attractive dried plant arrangement.
Try to do some weaving with the leaves.

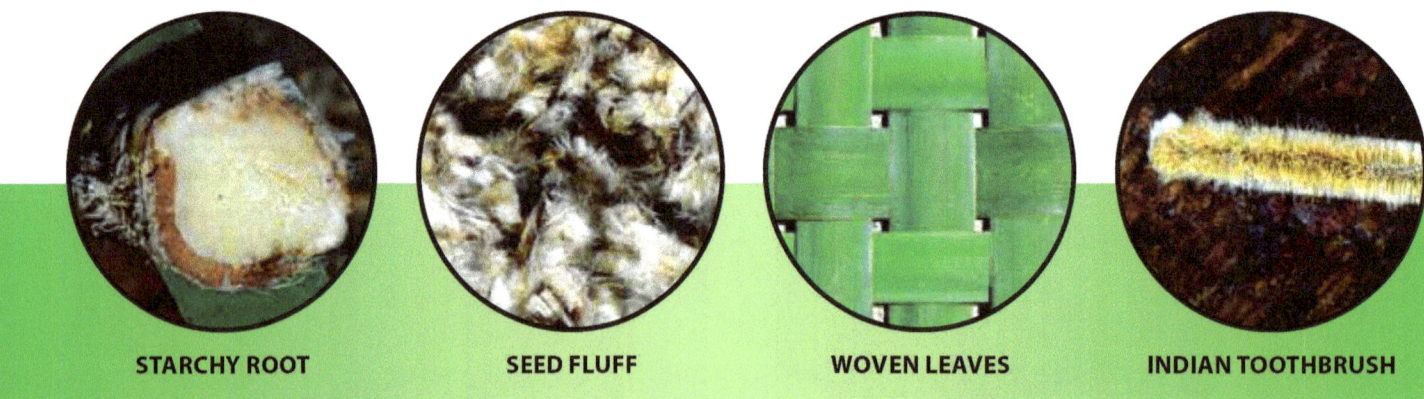

STARCHY ROOT **SEED FLUFF** **WOVEN LEAVES** **INDIAN TOOTHBRUSH**

Medicinal

The fluffy seed down is very soft and soothing when rubbed on skin rashes. However, some people are allergic to the seeds, and they may cause hives.

Indians rubbed stem juice on gums around achy teeth. They burned leaves and used the ashes as an antiseptic on wounds.

Edible parts are high in starch, vitamins A, B, and C, and potassium and phosphorus.

Ecology

The main animal users are muskrats - for building material and food, and birds – especially red wing blackbirds for nesting sites.

Colonies spread rapidly under water by the roots and rhizomes. Seeds start new colonies by landing in exposed mud.

They have been studied as a fuel source. Compressed fuel pellets burn readily, and the high starch content can be converted into alcohol.

As a shoreline plant, they stabilize the soil and filter impurities from the water.

SOLOMON'S SEAL 48

SOLOMON'S SEAL

Polygonatum biflorum
Family: Lily
May – July

Native

Other names
Lady Seals

Description
The long stem leans in a graceful arc, displaying oval leaves. Fragrant, pale green, bell shaped flowers hang in drooping clusters. They develop into pea size, blue violet berries.

How this plant came to be named after the Biblical King Solomon is somewhat a mystery (and perhaps a legend). It seems to be related to the creeping underground stem that displays a scar from each previous years main stem (by counting the scars, the age of the plant can be determined – one scar per year). The scars resemble the star- shaped seal on King Solomon's ring that he imprinted on important documents.

Edibility
Ripe berries were food for the Indians, but they sometimes caused vomiting. Birds eat them, and deer are fond of the leaves. Young shoots are boiled and eaten like asparagus.

Challenge
Watch for a similar plant – False Solomon's Seal, *Smilacina racemesa,* with star shaped creamy white flowers branching at the end of the stem. It produces edible ruby red berries that taste like molasses. Early settlers called them scurvy berries. Their apparent high Vitamin C content presumably prevented scurvy.

 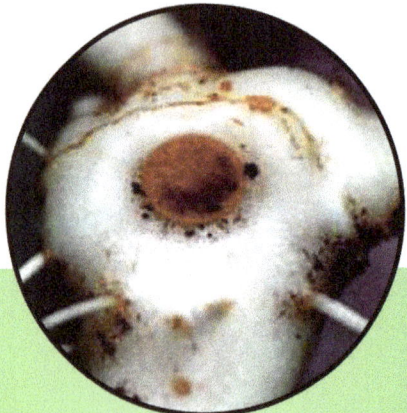 

SOLOMON'S RING SEAL **TWO YEAR RHIZOMES**

Medicinal
Dried, powdered roots made into a paste with water had many uses: healed bruises – removed freckles and acne, and was a popular skin cosmetic. As a tea, the root was used for menopause, indigestion, diabetes, insomnia, and kidney disorders. It can still be purchased as a healing herb in capsule form.

Ecology
The small flowers contain nectar which attracts bees, butterflies and hummingbirds. Young plants can be transplanted, and make an attractive ground cover – the leaves last all summer.

49 STINGING NETTLE

STINGING NETTLE

Urtica dioica
Family: Nettle
June – September

Alien – native to Europe

Other names
Hoky-poky
Hidgy-pidgy
Devils Play Thing
Burning Weed

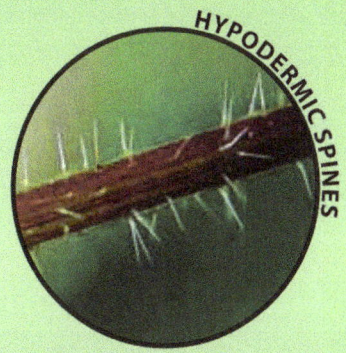

HYPODERMIC SPINES

Challenge
Without touching, look closely for the tiny, sharp, shiny needles on the stems and leaves.
Only for the brave and daring: Firmly grab the stem - it should not sting.
Locate some jewelweed, find the stem liquid, get stung by the nettles, apply the jewelweed juice - see how quickly the sting is relieved.
Note: If the above doesn't work – try to enjoy the "nettle high".

Description

If you don't find it, it may find you on almost any hike. Lightly brushing across the leaves produces an unforgettable, sudden sting, followed by white, itchy spots on the skin. The tiny, hypodermic needle-like spines lining the stems and leaves contain a complex mixture of histamines, acetylcholine, serotonin, and formic acid. The tiny needles perhaps function to keep the plant from annihilation by grazing animals, and perhaps humans, as young stinging nettles have a pleasant taste and are one of the most nutritious plants on earth. People vary in sensitivity, and some even find the sting invigorating, producing alertness – a "nettle high."

A technique known as flagellation was used on an unconscious person – near death, i.e. they were "flogged" with nettles in hopes of reviving them. Indians used the sting to stay awake on long journeys.

The worst sting is produced by lightly rubbing across the leaves with thin skin, such as the back of the hand or legs. "He that handles tenderly is soonest stung." In fact, grabbing the plant firmly may not even produce a sting. Perhaps there is a life lesson here: Confront problems firmly and directly. Don't lightly push them aside. Also, avoid "nettling" others.

If stung - there is an interesting variety of treatments:
1. Rub with saliva or urine.
2. Rub with nettle stem juice. The plant cures itself.
3. Wash quickly or rub with ice.
4. Cover sting with baking soda mixed with a little water.
5. Rub with juice from a jewelweed stem – works very well.
6. There are many drug store remedies.
7. Endure the pain and enjoy the "high."

It is a perennial, and grows up to three feet tall. The female plant has small green flowers that hang from the stem. The male flowers are more erect and near the top of the plant.

NETTLE LEAVES

NETTLE FLOWERS

Nettle was collected for the stem fibers – similar to hemp and flax – to make cloth. An excellent liquid fertilizer and insecticide can be made by soaking nettle plants in water.

Edibility
Nettle is considered delicious and very nutritious. It contains a variety of minerals including magnesium, potassium, and calcium and is high in vitamins A and C and protein. Heating or drying fresh leaves removes the sting. Dried or powdered, it is fed to a variety of animals: horses for shinier coats, cows – better milk, chickens – more eggs. It is used as an ingredient in many human skin and hair products. To use like spinach: wash – cook (no added water) for 20 minutes with lid on pan. It combines well with rice and beans. Collect young leaves (with gloves) in spring, or find new sprouts in the fall. Nettle tea is nourishing and stimulating.

Medicinal
Consuming nettles is excellent for building, restoring and detoxifying the liver, kidneys, muscles, adrenals, and prostate. It is a blood purifier, and boosts circulation. It relieves joint stiffness, muscle pain and sciatica, and relieves hay fever, allergies, and eczema. An old time remedy for rheumatism was to either whip the patient with nettle stems, or drop him naked into a nettle bed. The joint pain was either quickly cured or forgotten. Nettle capsules are available in health stores.

Ecology
The plant usually grows only on fertile soil, and prefers moist woodlands and shaded trails. The seeds are wind distributed, and young plants spread by underground stems. It is a host for the Red Admiral butterfly.

50 RAGWEED

RAGWEED FLOWER

RAGWEED

Common: Ambrosia artemisiifolia
Giant: Ambrosia trifida
Family: Composite
August – October

Native – has spread to Europe

Other names
Horseweed (Giant)
Bitter weed (Common)

HAY FEVER POLLEN

Description
There are two species - very different in appearance, yet they both cause the dreaded hay fever, which is suffered by 20% of the population .Unattractive, over-looked ragweed has managed to shift the hay fever blame to the showy, yellow flowering goldenrod, which blooms at the same time. However, goldenrod has heavy, sticky pollen carried by insects, not the wind, and is therefore not a factor in causing hay fever.

Common ragweed is up to three feet tall. Giant ragweed can be found over 15 feet tall (record- 18 feet, four inches). Both have separate male and female greenish flowers on the same plant, but they cannot self- pollinate. To insure that the wind will carry pollen to another plant, up to one billion pollen grains are released per plant, and are blown hundreds of miles, saturating the air. Sneezing means you have been "pollinated." This continues until frost kills the plant.

The bell shaped, upside down pollen producing male flowers are in clusters at the top of the plant. The tiny petal-less female flowers are at the base of the leaves. They produce spiny seeds that cling to fur and feathers.

Why the names ragweed and hay-fever? The leaves resemble torn rags and pollen is produced during the hay- making season. However, the pollen doesn't usually produce a fever.

Edibility
The seeds contain the essential fatty acid – linolenic acid. They are an important winter food source for birds. Deer and cattle graze on the leaves, which may cause a bitter taste in milk.

Challenge
Try to find both tall and common ragweed plants - they grow in the same area.
Pull the stem apart and find the tough fibers Indians used to make thread.
Look for the greenish male flowers on top and the female flowers along the stem.
Try not to get pollinated.

GIANT RAGWEED

COMMON RAGWEED

Medicinal
Indians found many uses for ragweed:

They rubbed crushed leaves on bites, stings, infections, and on skin to stop bleeding from a cut.

Leaf tea was used to treat fever and constipation.

Root tea treated menstrual problems.

They believed chewing on roots would alleviate fear at night.

Natural products for hay fever symptoms include:

Coenzyme Q10, quercetin, Vitamins A, B, C, alfalfa, yogurt, and foods high in magnesium: beans and green vegetables.

Ecology
The annual plants grow on uncultivated land and field edges. The best control is to pull out the plant before flowering. They can re-grow after being cut down as low as one half inch from the ground.

They can reduce corn and soybean yields by 50%.

ORANGE FLOWERS

Jewelweed

Butterfly Weed (refer to milkweed)

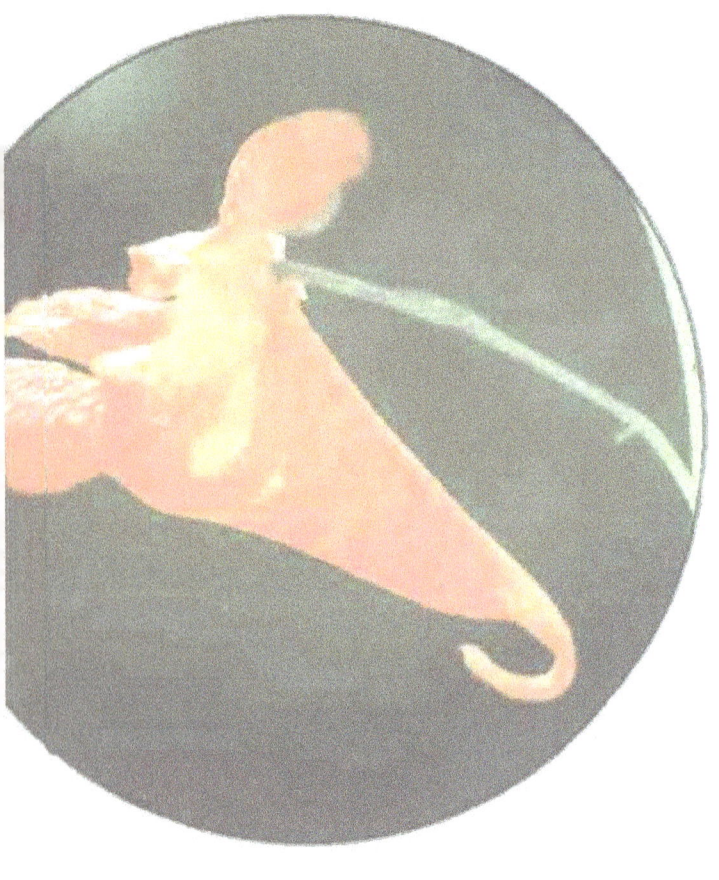

51 JEWELWEED

JEWELWEED

Impatiens capensis
Family: Touch-me-not
June – October

Native

Other names
Touch-Me-Not
Slipperweed

PALE JEWELWEED

SPOTTED JEWELWEED WITH WATER DROPLET "JEWELS"

Description
Jewelweed often lives in the company of poison ivy and stinging nettles. Appropriately, its stem juice will neutralize itching and stinging.

The trumpet shaped flowers are very bright and attractive, and resemble a necklace jewel. The leaf transforms rain drops into "diamonds." The fruit turns edible seeds into missiles. The stem provides a natural "Preparation H."

The flowers are either orange (*I. capensis*) or yellow (*I. pallida*). They grow up to five feet tall in dense colonies in shady, wet areas. The leaves are water - repellant and, when wet, form jewel-like droplets on the leaf surface. Contact with the mature, greenish-brown seed pods can be startling. If touched, they spring open and scatter seeds in all directions.

Edibility
Sprouts are edible up to six inches tall. Boil fifteen minutes in two changes of water. Seeds (blue inside with a brown covering) are small and hard to capture. They taste like walnuts. The foliage is relished by deer, and birds devour the seeds. The curved flower spur contains nectar, a favorite of humming birds and bees.

Medicinal
The stem, especially at the swollen nodes, contains a slippery fluid that is an effective skin tonic: used as a preventative and/or relief from poison ivy, nettle stings, mosquito bites, bruises, eczema, burns, sprains, warts, acne, athletes foot, headaches, etc. It contains the same active ingredients as Preparation H, and therefore, can be used in places where the "sun does not shine." Commercial preparations are available, or the juice can be obtained directly by breaking open the stem and rubbing into the affected area.

Challenge
Find a ripe, greenish or brownish pod and gently roll it between fingers. The pod will curl, twist and snap the seeds. Be careful of getting hit in the face. If you can catch them - taste the nutty flavor. Peel the seed coat to see the unusual blue color.
Hold leaves upside down under water. They will turn bright silver.

| SEEDLING | RIPE SEED POD | EXPLODED SEED POD |

Indians made a strong leaf tea as a preventative for poison ivy. The tea can be frozen into cubes, which are rubbed over infected skin. To make tea, plants are boiled at least 30 minutes until water turns orange (use orange jewelweed).

Ecology

The yellow species prefers dense shade, while the orange species adapts to disturbed areas, in semi-shade. They are annuals and can become invasive and hard to control.

There are two kinds of flowers on the same plant: The large open-petaled blooms are cross-pollinated and produce the explosive seed-pods. Small, closed flowers are self-pollinated.

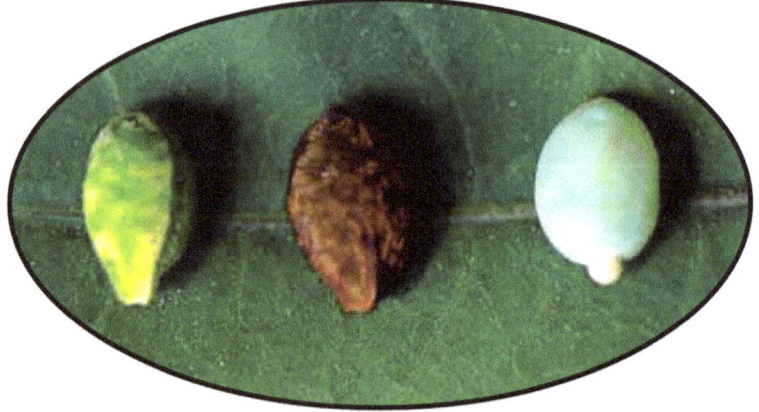

YOUNG SEED MATURE SEED BROWN COVER REMOVED

GLOSSARY

Annual: A plant that starts from seed, producing roots, stem, flowers and seeds, and dies in one growing season.

Biennial: A plant that produces roots and leaves the first year, survives the winter, then produces a stem, flowers and seeds the second year, then dies.

Bulb: An underground stem made up of thick scales surrounding a tiny plant.

Corm: Swollen, underground stem base, stores food over winter, and produces new leaves in spring.

Herbaceous: Soft stems without wood that die at end of summer.

Nectar: A sweet liquid produced by flower petals that attract insects and birds, resulting in pollination.

Node: The place on a plant stem where a leaf is attached.

Perennial: A plant that lasts for more than two growing seasons.

Pistil: The female flower part in the center of the flower which accepts pollen and produces eggs and seeds.

Pollen: Tiny, powder-like grains that contain sperm which fertilize the eggs formed in the pistils. It is carried by wind or insects.

Poultice: Crushed plant material applied directly to the skin, or covered with gauze and warmed before application.

Rhizome: A horizontal, underground stem that survives the winter and produces a new plant.

Sepal: Surrounds the petals, sometimes colorful- like the petals; sometimes green- like leaves. They protect the flower buds.

Stamen: The male part of a flower. They surround the pistil and produce pollen.

Tea infusion: Extracting the health promoting contents of a plant by soaking in water.

Tuber: An enlarged underground stem that has buds on the outside - like the "eyes" of a potato.

REFERENCES

Baker, Elizabeth and Baker, Dr. Elton. The Uncook Book. Indianola, WA: Derlwood Communications, 1980.

Barker, Joan. A Field Guide to the Wild Flowers of North America. China: Paragon Publishing Book, 2006.

Bremness, Lesley. Herbs. England: Darling Kindersley Ltd, 1999.

Brill, Steve / Dean, Evelyn. Identifying and Harvesting Edible and Medicinal Plants. New York: Harper Collins, 2002.

Brown, Tom Jr. Tom Brown's Guide to Wild Edible and Medicinal Plants. New York: Berkley Books, 1985.

Eastman, John. The Book of Swamp and Bog. PA: Stackpole Books, 1995.

Foster, Steven / Duke, James A. Eastern / Central Medicinal Plants - Peterson Field Guides, Boston: Houghton Mifflin, 1990

Fritchey, Philip. Practical Herbalism. Warsaw, Indiana: Wendell W. Whitman Co., 2004.

Gibbons, Euell. Stalking the Wild Asparagus. New York: David McKay Co. Inc., 1962.

Gibbons, Euell. Stalking the Healthful Herbs. New York: David McCay Co. Inc., 1966.

Harstad, Carolyn. Go Native. Bloomington, IN: Indiana University Press, 1999.

Heiser, Charles B. Weeds in My Garden. Portland, Oregon: Timber Press, 2003.

Horn, Dennis and Cathcart, Tavia. Wildflowers of Tennessee the Ohio Valley and the Southern Appalachians. Canada: Lone Pine Publishing. 2005.

Jackson, Marion T. The Natural Heritage of Indiana. Bloomington, IN: Indiana University Press, 1997.

Kowalchik, Claire, Hylton, William H. Rodales Illustrated Encyclopedia of Herbs. Emmaus, PA: Rodale Press, 1987.

Lyle, Katie. The Wild Berry Book. Claremont, ON: Northword Press, 1994.

Midgley, Jan W. Southeastern Wildflowers. Hong Kong: Cranehill Publishers, 1999.

Runkel, Sylvan T. / Bull, Alvin F. Wildflowers of Indiana Woodlands. Des Moines, Iowa: Wallace Homestead Book Co., 1979.

Sanders, Jack. The Secrets of Wildflowers. Guilford, CT: The Lyons Press, 2003

Tekiela, Stan. Wildflowers of Michigan Field Guide. Cambridge, MN: Adventure Publications, Inc., 2000.

Tekiela, Stan. Wildflowers of Ohio Field Guide. Cambridge, Minn.: Adventures Publications, Inc., 2001.

Thayer, Samuel. The Foragers Harvest. A Guide to Identifying, Harvesting, and Preparing Edible Wild Plants. Ogema, WI. 54459 Foragers Harvest, 2006.

Thieret, John W. / Niering, William A. / Olmstead, Nancy C. Field Guide to Wildflowers Eastern Region - Revised Edition. New York: Alfred A. Knopt, Inc.,1991.

Turner, Nancy J. / Szczawinski, Adam F. Common Poisonous Plants and Mushrooms of North America. Portland, Oregon: Timber Press, 1991.

Weil, Andrew, M.D. Spontaneous Healing. New York: Alfred A. Knopf, 1995.

Yatskievych, Kay. Field Guide to Indiana Wildflowers. Bloomington / Indianapolis. Indiana University Press. 2000.

REVIEWS

Contains more interesting facts about the plant varieties than any book I've read. The true to life photos make it easy to identify these plants in the wild.

Laura Lawson, Nature Enthusiast

Mr. Brenneman provides a masterful presentation for amateurs and experienced nature lovers. The book provides interesting facts about common plants found in the woods and fields. His photography offers excellent detail, and the information will bring great enjoyment and knowledge to all readers. It will establish a greater understanding and appreciation of wild plants.

Louis Feagans, School Administrator and photographer

www.ingramcontent.com/pod-product-compliance
Lightning Source LLC
LaVergne TN
LVHW072126060526
838201LV00071B/4984